Sepher Yetzirah

ספר יצירה

A BOOK ON CREATION;

THE JEWISH METAPHYSICS

OF

REMOTE ANTIQUITY

translated by Isidor Kalisch

[1877]

Hidden Mysteries
TGS Publishers

ספר יצירה

SEPHER YEZIRAH.
A BOOK ON CREATION

Translator: Isidor Kalisch
Historical Reprint, Alchemy, Creation, Religion, Judaism, Kabbalah

2006 TGS Publishers

ALL RIGHTS RESERVED. No part of this book may be reproduced in any form or by any means, electronic or mechanical, including photocopying, recording or by any information storage and retrieval system, without the written permission of the Publisher.

TGS Historical Reprint Series

TGS Publishers
22241 Pinedale Lane
Frankston, Texas 75763
903-876-3256
www.HiddenMysteries.com

Notice: TGS Publishers may or may not concur with the conclusions and theories of the author of this book. It is reprinted for its historical relevance and its controversial material. It is the sole responsibility of the readers to determine the veracity of the author's theories and research.

This book is a scanned project from an original copy of the book. Scanning errors may occur in the text and is considered normal and customary.

ספר יצירה׃

SEPHER YEZIRAH.

A BOOK ON CREATION;

OR,

THE JEWISH METAPHYSICS

OF

REMOTE ANTIQUITY.

With English Translation, Preface, Explanatory Notes and Glossary,

BY

Rev. Dr. ISIDOR KALISCH,

Author of the "Guide for Rational Inquiries into the Biblical Scriptures," "Toene des Morgenlandes," Translator of "Nathan the Wise" from the German, etc., etc., etc.

NEW YORK:
L. H. FRANK & CO., PUBLISHERS AND PRINTERS,
No. 32½ Bowery.

1877.

CONTENTS

PREFACE.	9
SEPHER YEZIRAH.	17
CHAPTER I.	17
CHAPTER II.	29
CHAPTER III.	35
CHAPTER IV.	41
CHAPTER V.	53
CHAPTER VI.	65
NOTES.	73
GLOSSARY OF RABBINICAL WORDS.	87
The Aleph Bet	95
SEFER YETZIRAH Saaida Translation	97
I. CHAPTER ONE	99
II. Chapter Two.	101
III. Chapter Three.	105
IV. Chapter Four.	109
V. Chapter Five.	113
VI. Chapter Six.	115
VII. Chapter Seven.	119
VIII. Chapter Eight.	121
Commentary on Sefer Yetzirah	123
I. On the Origin of the World According to the Pythagoreans & the Sefer Yetzirah	125
II. On the Divine Epithets and the Aristotelian Categories.	129
III. On the "Closed" Numbers, Mothers, Doubles, & Simples:	137

- IV. On the Creation's "Witnesses" 139
- V. On the Geometrical "Whirlwind" of the Hebrew Letters 141
- VI. On the Rotation of the Letters and the Zodiac 143
- VII. On the Ethereal Realm and its Relation to Prophecy 147
- VIII. On the Geometry of Phonetics and the Order of the Alphabet 151
- IX. On the 231 Gates of Letter Permutation 153
- X. On the Crowning of the Letters 159

The Sefer Yetzirah G. Scholem Translation 161
- Chapter 1 163
- Chapter 2 167
- Chapter 3 169
- Chapter 4 171
- Chapter 5 175
- Chapter 6 179

THE SEPHER YETZIRAH Heidrick Translation 181
- Chapter One 183
- Chapter Two 189
- Chapter Three 193
- Chapter Four 199
- Chapter Five 207
- Chapter Six 215

Sepher Yetzirah Westcott Translation 221
- PREFACE NOTE 223
- INTRODUCTION 223
- CHAPTER I 235
- CHAPTER II 239
- CHAPTER III 241

CHAPTER IV	243
Supplement to Chapter IV	244
CHAPTER V	247
Supplement to Chapter V	248
CHAPTER VI	251
THE FIFTY GATES OF INTELLIGENCE	253
THE THIRTY-TWO PATHS OF WISDOM	257
Notes to THE SEPHER YETZIRAH	263
Notes to CHAPTER I	265
Notes to CHAPTER 2	271
Notes to CHAPTER III	273
Notes to CHAPTER IV	275
Notes to CHAPTER V	277
Notes to CHAPTER VI	279
Notes to the Thirty-Two Paths of Wisdom	281

Sepher Yetzirah   Book of Creation

PREFACE.

This metaphysical essay, called "Sepher Yezirah," (book on creation, or cosmogony,) which I have endeavored to render into English, with explanatory notes, is considered by all modem literati as the first philosophical book that ever was written in the Hebrew language. But the time of its composition and the name of its author have not yet been ascertained, despite of the most elaborate researches of renowned archaeologists. Some maintain that this essay is mentioned in the Talmud treatise Sanhedrin, p. 66 b. and ibid. 67 b. which passage is according to the commentary of Rashi, to treatise Erubin, p. 63 a., a reliable historical notice. Hence this book was known already in the second or at the beginning of the third century of the Christian Era. The historian, Dr. Graetz, tries to show very ingeniously in his work, entitled "Gnosticism," p. 104 and 110, that it was written in the early centuries of the Christian Church, especially when the ideas and views of the Gnostics were in vogue. This opinion, however, he afterwards revoked. (See Dr. Graetz's "History of the Jews," Vol. V, p. 315 in a note.)

Dr. Zunz, the Nestor of the Jewish Rabbis in Europe, maintains that we have to look for the genesis of the book "Yezirah" in the Geonic period, (700-1000), and that it was consequently composed in a

ספר יצירה

post-talmudical time. But if so, it is very strange that Saadjah Gaon, who lived in the tenth, and Judah Halevi, who lived in the twelfth century, represented the book "Yezirah" as a very ancient work. Therefore it seems to me, that Dr. Graetz had no sufficient cause to repudiate his assertion concerning the age of this book; because all the difficulties which he himself and others raised against his supposition, fall to the ground, when we consider that the most ancient works, holy as well as profane, had one and the same fate, namely, that from age to age more or less interpolations were made by copyists and commentators. Compare also Prof. Tenneman's "Grundriss der Geschichte der Philosophie," improved by Prof. Wendt, p. 207.

Tradition, which ascribes the authorship of this book to the patriarch Abraham, is fabulous, as can be proved by many reasons; but the idea that Rabbi Akiba, who lived about the beginning of the second century, composed the book "Yezirah," is very likely possible. Be this as it may, it is worth while to know the extravagant hypotheses which ancient Jewish philosophers and theologians framed as soon as they began to contemplate and to reason, endeavoring to combine oriental and Greek theories. Although there is an exuberance of weeds, we will find, nevertheless, many germs of truisms, which are of the greatest importance. A Christian theologian, Johann Friedrich von Meyer D.

D., remarked very truly in his German preface to the book "Yezirah," published in Leipzig, 1830: "This book is for two reasons highly important: in the first place, that the real Cabala, or mystical doctrine of the Jews, which must be carefully distinguished from its excrescences, is in close connection and perfect accord with the Old and New Testaments; and in the second place, that the knowledge of it is of great importance to the philosophical inquirers, and can not be put aside. Like a cloud permeated by beams of light which makes one infer that there is more light behind it, so do the contents of this book, enveloped in obscurity, abound in coruscations of thought, reveal to the mind that there is a still more effulgent light lurking somewhere, and thus inviting us to a further contemplation and investigation, and at the same time demonstrating the danger of a superficial investigation, which is so prevalent in modem times, rejecting that which can not be understood at first sight."

I shall now try to give a sketch of the system as it is displayed in the book "Yezirah," which forms a link in the chain of the ancient theoretical speculations of philosophers, who were striving to ascertain the truth mainly by reasoning a-priori, and who imagined that it is thus possible to permeate all the secrets of nature. It teaches that a first cause, eternal, all-wise, almighty and holy, is the

ספר יצירה

origin and the centre of the whole universe, from whom gradually all beings emanated. Thought, speech and action are an inseparable unity in the divine being; God made or created, is metaphorically expressed by the word: writing. The Hebrew language and its characters correspond mostly with the things they designate, and thus holy thoughts, Hebrew language and its reduction to writing, form a unity which produce a creative effect.[1]

The self-existing first cause called the creation into existence by quantity and quality; the former represented by ten numbers, (Sephiroth,) the latter by twenty-two letters, which form together thirty-two ways of the divine wisdom. Three of the twenty-two letters, namely, Aleph, Mem, Sheen, are the mothers, or the first elements, from which came forth the primitive matter of the world: air, water and fire, that have their parallel in man, (male and female): breast, body and head, and in the year: moisture, cold and heat. The other seven double and twelve[2] simple letters are then

---

[1] Thus for instance, they imagined that the name of Jehovah, יהוי, is by reversing the alphabet: מצפן (mzpz); mem signifies the letter jod, zaddi, the letter he, and pe, the letter wav. These unmeaning sounds, they said, have magic power. Some maintained that the Hebrew language consists of twenty-two consonants, because being the complex of all beings, its number is equal to the most perfect figure, namely, of the periphery, as it is well known that the diameter is always to the periphery as seven to twenty-two.

[2] It was frequently observed by Jewish and Christian theologians, that the Marcosianio Gnostic system, as well as that of the Clementinians of the second century, contain

Sepher Yetzirah — Book of Creation

represented as stamina, from which other spheres or media of existence emanated.

Man is a microcosm, as the neck separates rationality from vitality, so does diaphragm the vitality from the vegetativeness. God stands in close connection with the Universe, and just so is Tali connected with the world, that is, an invisible, celestial or universal axis carries the whole fabric. In the year by the sphere, in man by the heart, and thus is the ruling spirit of God everywhere. Notwithstanding the decay of the individual, the genus is produced by the antithesis of man and wife.

Hebrew commentaries on the book "Yezirah" were composed by: first, Saadjah Gaon, of Fajum in Egypt, (892-942); second, Rabbi Abraham ben Dior Halevi; third, Rabbi Moses ben Nachman; fourth, Elieser of Germisa; fifth, Moses Botarel; sixth, Rabbi Eliah Wilna: The book "Yezirah," together with all these commentaries, was published in 1860, in the city of Lemberg. But although the commentator Saadjah was a sober minded scholar in a superstitious age, a good Hebrew grammarian, a renowned theologian and a

---

many analogies and parallels with the book "Yezirah." Marcus divides the Greek alphabet into three parts, namely: nine mute consonants ἄφωνα, eight half vowels ἡμίφωνα, and seven vowels φωνήεντα, in order to give a clear idea of the peculiar constitution of his "Aeons." (Irenaeus Haer, I, 16.)

ספר יצירה

good translator of the Hebrew Pentateuch, Isaiah and Job into the Arabian language, his ideas and views were, nevertheless, very often much benighted. See his comments on Yez. Chap. I, etc., etc.; his notes on "Yezirah" Chap. III, 2, prove undoubtedly that he had no knowledge whatever of natural science, and therefore his annotations on the book "Yezirah" are of little or no use at all. All the other commentaries mentioned above, together with all quotations of other expounders of the same book, contain nothing but a medley of arbitrary, mystical explanations and sophistical distortions of scriptural verses, astrological notions, oriental superstitions, a metaphysical jargon, a poor knowledge of physics and not a correct elucidation of the ancient book; they drew mostly from their own imagination, and credited the author of "Yezirah" with saying very strange things which he never thought of. I must not omit to mention two other Hebrew commentaries, one by Judah Halevi, and the other by Ebn Ezra, who lived in the first part of the twelfth century. They succeeded in explaining the book "Yezirah" in a sound scientific manner, but failed in making themselves generally understood, on account of the superstitious age in which they lived, and the tenacity with which the people in that period adhered to the marvelous and supernatural; they found, therefore, but few followers, and the 'book "Yezirah" remained to the public an enigma and an ancient curiosity, giving rise to a system of metaphysical delirium, called Cabala.

Translations of the book "Yezirah" and comments thereon by learned Christian authors are: first, a translation of the book "Yezirah" with explanatory notes in the Latin language, by Wilhelm Postellus, Paris, France, 1552; second, another Latin version is contained in Jo. Pistorii artis cabalistical scriptorum, Tom I, p. 869, sqq., differing from that of Postellus. Some are of the opinion that John Reuchlin, while others maintain that Paul Riccius was the author of it. (See Wolfii Biblioth. Hebr. Tom., I, Chap. 1.) Third, Rittangel published the book "Yezirah," 1642, at Amsterdam, entitled: "Liber Yezirah qui Abrahamo patriarchae adscribitur, una cum commentario Rabbi Abraham F. D. (filii Dior) super 32 Semitis Sapientiae, a quibus liber Yezirah incipit. Translatus et notis illustrates, a Joanne Stephano Rittangelio, ling. Orient. in Elect. Acad. Regiomontana Prof. extraord. Amstelodami ap. Jo. and Jodoc. Janssonios," 1642, in quarto; fourth, Johann Friedrich von Mayer, D. D., published the book "Yezirah" in Hebrew with a translation and explanatory notes in the German language, Leipzig, 1830.

All these translations are out of print and are rarely found even in well regulated libraries. I was so fortunate as to obtain a copy of Dr.

ספר יצירה

Mayer's edition of the book "Yezirah." He states in the preface to it, that he had a copy of Postellus' translation in manuscript as well as some others, and compared them. The explanatory notes given by this author are, nevertheless, insufficient and sometimes very incorrect. The present translation is, as far as I could ascertain, the first that was ever published in the English language. Again, I have to add that I have not only endeavored to correct a great many mistakes and erroneous ideas of my predecessors, but I have also endeavored to give more complete annotations. I therefore hope that the candid reader will consider the great difficulties I had to overcome in this still unbeaten way of the ancient Jewish spiritual region, and will receive with indulgence this new contribution to archaeological knowledge.

DR. ISIDOR KALISCH.

Sepher Yetzirah   *Book of Creation*

SEPHER YEZIRAH.

CHAPTER I.

SECTION 1.

Yah,[1] the Lord of hosts, the living God, King of the Universe, Omnipotent, All-Kind and Merciful, Supreme and Extolled, who is Eternal, Sublime and Most-Holy, ordained (formed) and created the Universe in thirty-two[2] mysterious paths[3] of wisdom by three[4] Sepharim, namely: 1) S'for סְפָר; 2) Sippur סִפּוּר; and 3) Sapher סֵפֶר which are in Him one and the same. They consist of a decade out of nothing[5] and of twenty-two fundamental letters. He divided the twenty-two consonants into three divisions: 1) three אמ ות mothers, fundamental letters or first elements; 2) seven double; and 3) twelve simple consonants.

ספר יצירה

ספר יצירה.

פרק ראשון.

משנה א.

בִּשְׁלֹשִׁים וּשְׁתַּיִם נְתִיבוֹת פְּלִיאוֹת חָכְמָה חָקַק יָהּ יְהֹוָ"ה צְבָאוֹת אֱלֹהֵ"י יִשְׂרָאֵל אֱלֹהִים חַיִּים וּמֶלֶךְ עוֹלָם אֵל שַׁדַּי רַחוּם וְחַנּוּן רָם וְנִשָּׂא שׁוֹכֵן עַד מָרוֹם וְקָדוֹשׁ שְׁמוֹ וּבָרָא אֶת עוֹלָמוֹ בִּשְׁלֹשָׁה סְפָרִים *בִּסְפָר וּסְפוֹר וְסֵפֶר: עֶשֶׂר סְפִירוֹת בְּלִימָה וְעֶשְׂרִים וּשְׁתַּיִם אוֹתִיּוֹת יְסוֹד: שָׁלֹשׁ אִמּוֹת וְשֶׁבַע כְּפוּלוֹת וּשְׁתֵּים עֶשְׂרֵה פְשׁוּטוֹת:

*) נ"א. בְּסֵפֶר וְסוֹפֵר וְסִפּוּר:

SECTION 2.

The decade [6] out of nothing is analogous to that of the ten fingers (and toes) of the human body, five parallel to five, and in the centre of which is the covenant with the only One, by the word of the tongue and the rite of Abraham.

SECTION 3.

Ten are the numbers out of nothing, and not the number nine, ten and not eleven. Comprehend this great wisdom, understand this [7] knowledge, inquire into it and ponder on it, render it evident and lead [8] the Creator back to His throne again.

ספר יצירה
משנה ב.

עֶשֶׂר סְפִירוֹת בְּלִימָה כְּמִסְפַּר עֶשֶׂר אֶצְבָּעוֹת חָמֵשׁ כְּנֶגֶד חָמֵשׁ וּבְרִית יָחִיד מְכֻוֶּנֶת בָּאֶמְצַע בְּמִלַּת הַלָּשׁוֹן וּבְמִלַּת הַמָּעוֹר:

משנה ג.

עֶשֶׂר סְפִירוֹת בְּלִימָה עֶשֶׂר וְלֹא תֵּשַׁע עֶשֶׂר וְלֹא אַחַת עֶשְׂרֵה הָבֵן בְּחָכְמָה וַחֲכַם בְּבִינָה בְּחוֹן בָּהֶם חֲקוֹר מֵהֶם וְהַעֲמֵד דָּבָר עַל בּוּרְיוֹ וְהוֹשֵׁב יוֹצֵר עַל-מְכוֹנוֹ:

SECTION 4.

The decade out of nothing has the following ten infinitudes:

1) The beginning ^{9} infinite.   6) The depth infinite.

2) " end "   7) " East "

3) " good "   8) " West "

4) " evil ^{10} "   9) " North "

5) " height "   10) " South "

and the only Lord God, the faithful King, rules over all from His holy habitation for ever and ever.

SECTION 5.

The appearance of the ten spheres out of nothing is like a flash of lightning, being without an end, His word is in them, when they go and return; they run by His order like a whirlwind and humble themselves before His throne.

ספר יצירה

משנה ד.

עֶשֶׂר סְפִירוֹת בְּלִימָה מִדָּתָן עֶשֶׂר שֶׁאֵין לָהֶם סוֹף עוֹמֶק רֵאשִׁית וְעוֹמֶק אַחֲרִית עוֹמֶק טוֹב וְעוֹמֶק רָע עוֹמֶק רוֹם וְעוֹמֶק תַּחַת עוֹמֶק מִזְרָח וְעוֹמֶק מַעֲרָב עוֹמֶק צָפוֹן וְעוֹמֶק דָּרוֹם אָדוֹן יָחִיד אֵל מֶלֶךְ נֶאֱמָן מוֹשֵׁל בְּכֻלָּם מִמְּעוֹן קָדְשׁוֹ עַד עֲדֵי עַד:

משנה ה.

עֶשֶׂר סְפִירוֹת בְּלִימָה צְפִיָּיתָן כְּמַרְאֵה הַבָּזָק וְתַכְלִיתָן אֵין לָהֶן קֵץ דְּבָרוֹ בָהֶן בְּרָצוֹא וָשׁוֹב וְלְמַאֲמָרָן כְּסוּפָה יִרְדּוֹפוּ וְלִפְנֵי כִסְאוֹ הֵם מִשְׁתַּחֲוִים:

SECTION 6

The decade of existence out of nothing has its end linked to its beginning and its beginning linked to its end, just as the flame is wedded to the live coal; because the Lord is one and there is not a second one, and before one what wilt thou count? [11]

SECTION 7.

Concerning the number ten of the spheres of existence out of nothing keep thy tongue from speaking and thy mind from pondering on it, and if thy mouth urges thee to speak, and thy heart to think about it, return! as it reads: "And the living creatures ran and returned," (Ezekiel 1,14.) and upon this [12] was the covenant made.

ספר יצירה

משנה ו.

עֶשֶׂר סְפִירוֹת בְּלִימָה נָעוּץ סוֹפָן בַּתְחִלָּתָן וּתְחִלָּתָן בְּסוֹפָן כְּשַׁלְהֶבֶת קְשׁוּרָה* בְּגַחֶלֶת שֶׁאָדוֹן יָחִיד וְאֵין לוֹ שֵׁנִי וְלִפְנֵי אֶחָד מַה אַתָּה סוֹפֵר:

*) רַבֵּינוּ הַאי" נָאוֹן ז"ל כָּתַב בְּסֵפֶר הַקְּמִיצָה וו"ל כָּתַב בַּעַל סֵפֶר יְצִירָה בְּשַׁלְהֶנֶת שׁוֹרָה בְּנַחֶלֶת:

משנה ז.

עֶשֶׂר סְפִירוֹת בְּלִימָה בְּלוֹם פִּיךָ מִלְּדַבֵּר וְלִבְּךָ מִלְּהַרְהֵר וְאִם רָץ פִּיךָ לְדַבֵּר לְהַרְהֵר שׁוּב לִמְקוֹם שֶׁלְּכָךְ נֶאֱמַר וְהַחַיּוֹת רָצוֹא וָשׁוֹב וְעַל דָּבָר זֶה נִכְרַת בְּרִית:

SECTION 8.

The following are the ten categories of existence out of nothing:

1) The spirit of the living God, praised and glorified be the name of Him who lives to all eternity. The articulate word of creative power, the spirit and the word are what we call the holy spirit is

2) Air emanated from the spirit by which He formed and established twenty-two consonants, stamina. Three of them, however, are fundamental letters, or mothers, seven double and twelve simple consonants; hence the spirit is the first one.

3) Primitive water emanated from the air. He formed and established by it Bohu [14] (water, stones) mud and loam, made them like a bed, put them up like a wall, and surrounded them as with a rampart, put coldness upon them and they became dust, as it reads: "He says to the snow (coldness) be thou earth." (Job 37, 6.)

4) Fire or ether emanated from the water. He established by it the throne of glory, the Seraphim and Ophanim, the holy living creatures and the angels, and of these three He formed His habitation, as it reads: "Who made His angels spirits, His ministers a flaming fire." (Psalm 104, 4.) He selected three consonants from the simple ones which are in the hidden secret of three mothers or first elements: ש-מ-א, air, water and ether or fire. He sealed them with spirit and fastened them to His great name and sealed with it six dimensions. [15]

ספר יצירה

משנה ח.

עֶשֶׂר סְפִירוֹת בְּלִימָה אַחַת רוּחַ אֱלֹהִים חַיִּים
בָּרוּךְ וּמְבוֹרָךְ שְׁמוֹ שֶׁל חַי הָעוֹלָמִים קוֹל וְרוּחַ
וְדִבּוּר וְהוּא רוּחַ הַקּוֹדֶשׁ: שְׁתַּיִם רוּחַ מֵרוּחַ חָקַק
וְחָצַב בָּהּ עֶשְׂרִים וּשְׁתַּיִם אוֹתִיּוֹת יְסוֹד שָׁלשׁ אִמּוֹת
וְשֶׁבַע כְּפוּלוֹת וּשְׁתֵּים עֶשְׂרֵה פְּשׁוּטוֹת וְרוּחַ אַחַת
מֵהֶן: שָׁלשׁ מַיִם מֵרוּחַ חָקַק וְחָצַב בָּהֶן (עֶשְׂרִים
וּשְׁתַּיִם אוֹתִיּוֹת) תֹּהוּ וָבֹהוּ רֶפֶשׁ וָטִיט חֲקָקָן כְּמִין
עֲרוּגָה הַצִּיבָן* כְּמִין חוֹמָה סְכָכָם** כְּמִין מַעֲזִיבָה
(וַיִּצַק עֲלֵיהֶם שֶׁלֶג וְנַעֲשָׂה עָפָר שֶׁנֶּאֱמַר כִּי לַשֶּׁלֶג
יֹאמַר הֱוֵא אָרֶץ): אַרְבַּע אֵשׁ מִמַּיִם חָקַק וְחָצַב בָּהּ
כִּסֵּא הַכָּבוֹד שְׂרָפִים וְאוֹפַנִּים? וְהַיּוֹת הַקּוֹדֶשׁ וּמַלְאֲכֵי
יֹאמַר הֱוֵא אָרֶץ): אַרְבַּע אֵשׁ מִמַּיִם חָקַק וְחָצַב בָּהּ
כִּסֵּא הַכָּבוֹד שְׂרָפִים וְאוֹפַנִּים? וְהַיּוֹת הַקּוֹדֶשׁ וּמַלְאֲכֵי
הַשָּׁרֵת וּמִשְּׁלָשְׁתָּן יָסַד מְעוֹנוֹ שֶׁנֶּאֱמַר עוֹשֶׂה
מַלְאָכָיו רוּחוֹת מְשָׁרְתָיו אֵשׁ לוֹהֵט בִּירַר שְׁלֹשָׁה
אוֹתִיּוֹת מִן הַפְּשׁוּטוֹת בְּסוֹד שָׁלשׁ אִמּוֹת א"מ"ש***
וּקְבָעָם בִּשְׁמוֹ הַגָּדוֹל וְחָתַם בָּהֶם שֵׁשׁ קְצָווֹת:

*) נוסחא אחרינא: הִצְבָן:

**) נ"א סִיבְּכָן:

***) יש הוסיף: הָתַם וָה"ה בְּעַד שָׁלשׁ:

5) He sealed the height and turned towards above, and sealed it with יהו

6) He sealed the depth, turned towards below and sealed it with היו

7) He sealed the east and turned forward, and sealed it with ויה

8) He Sealed the west and turned backward, and sealed it with והי

9) He sealed the south and turned to the right and sealed it with יוה

10) He sealed the north and turned to the left and sealed it with הוי

SECTION 9.

These are the ten spheres of existence out of nothing. From the spirit of the living God emanated air, from the air, water, from the water, fire or ether, from the ether, the height and the depth, the East and West, the North and South.

ספר יצירה

חָמֵשׁ חָתַם רוֹם וּפָנָה לְמַעְלָה וְחָתְמוֹ   בִּיהוּ

שֵׁשׁ חָתַם תַּחַת וּפָנָה לְמַטָּה וְחָתְמוֹ   בְּהיוּ

שֶׁבַע חָתַם מִזְרָח וּפָנָה לְפָנָיו וְחָתְמוֹ   בּוֹיה

שְׁמוֹנָה חָתַם מַעֲרָב וּפָנָה לְאַחֲרָיו וְחָתְמוֹ   בוֹהי

תֵּא_ע חָתַם דָּרוֹם וּפָנָה לִימִינוֹ וְחָתְמוֹ   בִּיוה

אֲשֶׁר חָתַם צָפוֹן וּפָנָה לִשְׂמֹאל לוֹ וְחָתְמוֹ   בּהוֹי

משנה ט.

אֵלוּ עֶשֶׂר סְפִירוֹת בְּלִימָה אַחַת רוּחַ אֱלֹהִים חַיִּים רוּחַ מֵרוּחַ מַיִם מֵרוּחַ אֵשׁ מִמַּיִם רוּם וְתַחַת מִזְרָח וּמַעֲרָב צָפוֹן וְדָרוֹם:

CHAPTER II.

SECTION 1.

There are twenty-two letters, stamina. Three of them, however, are the first elements, fundamentals or mothers, seven double and twelve simple consonants. The three fundamental letters א-מ-ש have as their basis the balance. In one scale [17] is the merit and in the other criminality, which are placed in equilibrium by the tongue. The three fundamental letters א-מ-ש signify, as מ is mute like the water and ש hissing like the fire, there is א among them, a breath of air which reconciles them.

SECTION 2.

The twenty-two letters which form the stamina after having been appointed and established by God, He combined, weighed and changed them, and formed by them all beings which are in existence, and all those which will be formed in all time to come.

ספר יצירה

פרק שני.

משנה א.

עֶשְׂרִים וּשְׁתַּיִם אוֹתִיּוֹת יְסוֹד שָׁלֹשׁ אִמּוֹת וְשֶׁבַע כְּפוּלוֹת וּשְׁתֵּים עֶשְׂרֵה פְּשׁוּטוֹת שָׁלֹשׁ אִמּוֹת אַיֵּ״מֵּשׁ יְסוֹדָן כַּף זְכוּת וְכַף חוֹבָה וְלָשׁוֹן חֹק מַכְרִיעַ בֵּנְתַיִם שָׁלֹשׁ אִמּוֹת אַיֵּ״מֵּשׁ מִי דוֹמֶמֶת שִׁי שׁוֹרֶקֶת אִי אֲוִיר רוּחַ מַכְרִיעַ בֵּנְתַיִם:

משנה ב.

עֶשְׂרִים וּשְׁתַּים אוֹתִיּוֹת יְסוֹד חֲקָקָן חֲצָבָן צְרָפָן שְׁקָלָן וְהֵמִירָן וְצָר בָּהֶם אֶת כָּל הַיְצוּר וְאֶת כָּל הֶעָתִיד לָצוּר:

SECTION 3.

He established twenty-two letters, stamina, by the voice, formed by the breath of air and fixed them on five places in the human mouth, namely: 1) gutturals, אהחצ 2) palatals, גיכק 3) linguals, דטלנת 4) dentals, זשסרץ 5) labials, מפבו.

SECTION 4.

He fixed the twenty-two letters, stamina, on the sphere like a wall with two hundred and thirty-one gates, [18] and turned the spheres forward and backward. For an illustration may serve the three letters, צנג. There is nothing better than joy, and nothing worse than sorrow or plague is. [19]

ספר יצירה

משנה ג.

עֶשְׂרִים וּשְׁתַּיִם אוֹתִיּוֹת יְמוֹד חֲקָקָן בְּקוֹל חָצְבָן בְּרוּחַ קְבָעָן בְּפֶה בְּחָמֵשׁ מְקוֹמוֹת אוֹתִיּוֹת אחה״ע בְּגָרוֹן גיכ״ק בַּחֵיךְ דטלנ״ת בַּלָּשׁוֹן זשסר״ץ בְּשִׁנַּיִם בומ״ף בִּשְׂפָתַיִם:

משנה ד.

עֶשְׂרִים וּשְׁתַּיִם אוֹתִיּוֹת יְסוֹד קְבָעָן בְּגַלְגַּל בְּמִין חוֹמָה ברל״א שְׁעָרִים וְחוֹזֵר הַגַּלְגַּלִים פָּנִים וְאָחוֹר וְסִימָן לַדָּבָר אֵין בְּטוֹבָה לְמַעְלָה מֵעֹנֶג וְאֵין בְּרָעָה לְמַטָה מִנֶּגַע:

SECTION 5.

But how was it done? He combined, [20] weighed and changed: the א with all the other letters in succession, and all the others again with א; ב with all, and all again with ב ; and so the whole series of letters. [21] Hence it follows that there are two hundred and thirty-one [22] formations, and that every creature and every word emanated from one names. [23]

SECTION 6.

He created a reality out of nothing, called the nonentity into existence and hewed, as it were, colossal pillars from intangible air. This has been shown by the example of combining the letter א with all the other letters, and all the other letters with Aleph (א). He [24] predetermined, and by speaking created every creature and every word by one name. For an illustration may serve the twenty-two elementary substances by the primitive substance of Aleph [25] (א).

ספר יצירה

משנה ה.

בֵּיצַד צְרָפָן שְׁקָלָן וְהֵמִירָן א עִם כֻּלָּן וְכֻלָּן עִם א ב עִם כֻּלָּן וְכֻלָּן עִם ב נְחוֹוְרוֹת חֲלִילָה וְנִמְצָאוֹת ברל״א שְׁעָרִים וְנִמְצָא כָּל הַיְצוּר וְכָל הַדִבּוּר יוֹצֵא מִשֵּׁם* אֶחָד:

*) נ״א בְּשֵׁם:

משנה ו.

יָצַר מַמָּשׁ מִתַּשׁ מִתֹּה ו וְעָשָׂה אֶת אֵינוֹ יֶשְׁנוֹ וְחָצַב עַמּוּדִים גְּדוֹלִים מֵאֲוִיר שֶׁאֵינוֹ נִתְפָּם וְזֶה סִימָן אוֹת א עִם כֻּלָּן נִכְלָן עִם א צוֹפֶה וּמֵמִיר וְעָשָׂה אֶת כָּל הַיְצוּר וְאֶת כָּל הַדִבּוּר שֵׁם אֶחָד וְסִימָן לַדָּבָר עֶשְׂרִים וּשְׁתַּיִם חֲפָצִים בְּגוּף א:

CHAPTER III.

SECTION 1.

The three first elements, א-מ-ש are typified by a balance, in one scale the merit and in the other the criminality, which are placed in equilibrium by the tongue. These three mothers, א-מ-ש are a great, wonderful and unknown mystery, and are sealed by six [26] rings, or elementary circles, namely: air, water and fire emanated from them, which gave birth to progenitors, and these progenitors gave birth again to some offspring.

SECTION 2.

God appointed and established the three mothers, א-מ-ש combined, weighed and changed them, and formed by them three mothers א-מ-ש in the world, in the year and in man, male and female.

ספר יצירה
פרק שלישי.

משנה א.

שָׁלשׁ אִמּוֹת אָמָ"שׁ יְסוֹדָן כַּף זְכוּת וְכַף חוֹבָה וְלָשׁוֹן חַק מַכְרִיעַ בְּנְתַיִם שָׁלשׁ אִמּוֹת אָמָ"שׁ סוֹד גָּדוֹל מוּפְלָא וּמְכוּסָה וְחָתוּם בְּשֵׁשׁ טַבָּעוֹת וְיָצְאוּ* מֵהֶם אֲוִיר וּמַיִם וְאֵשׁ וּמֵהֶם נוֹלְדוּ אָבוֹת וּמֵאָבוֹת תּוֹלְדוֹת:

*) נ"יא וּמִמֶּנּוּ יוֹצְאִים אֵשׁ וּמַיִם וּמִתְחַלְּקִים זָכָר וּנְקֵבָה שָׁלשׁ אִמּוֹת אָמָ"שׁ יְסוֹדָן וּמֵהֶן נוֹלוּ אָבוֹת שֶׁמִּמֶּנּוּ נִבְרָא הַכֹּל:

משנה ב.

שָׁלשׁ אִמּוֹת אָמָ"שׁ חַקְקָן חָצְבָן צָרְפָן שְׁקָלָן וְהֶחֱלִיפָן וְצָר בָּהֶם שָׁלשׁ אִמּוֹת אָמָ"שׁ בָּעוֹלָם וְשָׁלשׁ אִמּוֹת אָמָ"שׁ בַּשָּׁנָה וְשָׁלשׁ אִמּוֹת אָמָ"שׁ בַּנֶּפֶשׁ זָכָר וּנְקֵבָה:

SECTION 3.

The three mothers ש-מ-א in the world are: air, water and fire. Heaven was created from fire or ether; the earth (comprising sea and land) from the elementary water; and the atmospheric air from the elementary air, or spirit, which establishes the balance among them.

SECTION 4.

The three mothers ש-מ-א produce in the year [27]: heat, coldness [28] and moistness. Heat was created from fire, coldness from water, and moistness from air which equalizes them.

SECTION 5.

The three mothers ש-מ-א produce in man, male and female, breast, body and head. The head was created from fire, the breast from water, and the body from air, which places them in equilibrium.

ספר יצירה
משנה ג.

שָׁלֹשׁ אִמּוֹת אֶ״מִ״שׁ בָּעוֹלָם אֲוִיר וּמַיִם וְאֵשׁ שָׁמַיִם
נִבְרְאוּ מֵאֵשׁ וְאֶרֶץ נִבְרֵאת מִמַּיִם וְאַוִיר מֵרוּחַ
מַכְרִיעַ בֵּנְתַיִם:

משנה ג.

שָׁלֹשׁ אִמּוֹת אֶ״מִ״שׁ בַּשָּׁנָה חוֹם וְקוֹר וּרְוָיָה חוֹם
נִבְרָא מֵאֵשׁ קוֹר נִבְרָא מִמַּיִם וּרְוָיָה מַכְרִיעַ
בֵּנְתוֹם:

משנה ה.

שָׁלֹשׁ אִמּוֹת אֶ״מִ״שׁ בַּנֶּפֶשׁ זָכָר בִּנְקֵבָה ר אֵשׁ וּבֶטֶן
וּגְוִיָּה ר אֵשׁ נִבְרָא מֵאֵשׁ וּבֶטֶן נִבְרָא מִמַּרם וּגְוִיָּה
מֵרוּחַ מַכְרִיעַ בֵּנְתַיִם:

SECTION 6.

FIRST DIVISION. God let the letter. Aleph (א) predominate in primitive air, crowned [29] it, combined one with the other, [30] and formed by them the air in the world, moisture in the year, and the breast in man, male and female; in male by א-מ-ש and in female by א-ש-ם :

SECTION 7.

SECOND DIVISION. He let the letter Mem (מ) predominate in primitive water, and crowned it, combined one with the other, and formed by them the earth, (including land and sea) coldness in the year, and the belly in male and female; in male by א-מ-ש [31], in female by מ-ש-א

SECTION 8.

THIRD DIVISION. He let the letter Sheen (ש) predominate in primitive fire, crowned it, combined one with the other, and formed by them, heaven in the world, heat in the year, and the head of male and female. [32]

ספר יצירה

משנה ו.

בָּבָא א. הִמְלִיךְ אוֹת א' בְּרוּחַ וְקָשַׁר לוֹ כֶּתֶר וְצָרְפָן זֶה בָזֶה וְצָר בָּהֶם אֲוִיר בָּעוֹלָם רְוָיָה בַּשָּׁנָה וְוָיָה בַּנֶּפֶשׁ זָכָר בְּאֶ"מִ"יש ונקבה בְּאִ"יֹ"שם:

משנה ז.

בָּבָא ב. הִמְלִיךְ אוֹת מ' בְּמַיִם וְקָשַׁר לוֹ כֶּתֶר וְצָרְפָן זֶה בָזֶה נָצַר בָּהֶם אֶרֶץ בָּעוֹלָם וְקוֹר בַּשָּׁנָה וּבֶטֶן בַּנֶּפֶשׁ זָכָר בְּאֶ"מִ"יש* וּנְקֵבָה בְּמַ"יְ"שא:

*) נִיא בְּמֶ"יאִ"יש:

משנה ח.

בָּבָא ג. הִמְלִיךְ אוֹת שׁ' בְּאֵשׁ וְקָשַׁר לוֹ כֶּתֶר וְצָרְפָן זֶה בָזֶה וְצָר בָּהֶם שָׁמַיִם בָּעוֹלָם וְחוֹם בַּשָּׁנָה וָר אֵשׁ בַּנֶּפֶשׁ זָכָר וּנְקֵבָה:

CHAPTER IV.

SECTION 1.

The [33] seven double letters, בגד כפרת with a duplicity of pronunciation, aspirated and unaspirated, namely: כּכ, פּפ, תּת,‏ הּר, דּד, גּג, בּב serve as a model of softness and hardness, strength and weakness.

SECTION 2.

Seven [34] double letters, בגד כפרת shall, as it were, symbolize wisdom, wealth, fruitfulness, life, dominion, peace and beauty.

SECTION 3.

Seven double letters serve to signify the antithesis to which human life is exposed. The antithesis of wisdom is foolishness; of wealth, poverty; of fruitfulness, childlessness; of life, death; of dominion, dependence; of peace, war; and of beauty, ugliness.

ספר יצירה
פרק רביעי.

משנה א.
שֶׁבַע כְּפוּלוֹת בְּגָ״ד כַּפְרָ״ת מִתְנַהֲגוֹת בִּשְׁתֵּי לְשׁוֹנוֹת בָּ״ב גָּ״ג דָּ״ד כָּ״ךְ פָּ״פ רָּ״ר תָּ״ת תַּבְנִית רַךְ וְקָשֶׁה גִּבּוֹר וְחַלָּשׁ:

משנה ב.
שֶׁבַע כְּפוּלוֹת בְּגָ״ד כַּפְרָ״ת יְסוֹדָן חָכְמָה וְעוֹשֶׁר זֶרַע וְהַחַיִּים וּמֶמְשָׁלָה שָׁלוֹם וְחֵן:

משנה ג.
שֶׁבַע כְּפוּלוֹת בְּגָ״ד כַּפְרָ״ת כַּרְבּוּר וּבִתְמוּרָה תְּמוּרַת הַחָכְמָה אִוֶּלֶת תְּמוּרַת עֹשֶׁר עֹנִי תְּמוּרַת זֶרַע שְׁמָמָה תְּמוּרַת הַחַיִּים מָוֶת תְּמוּרַת מֶמְשָׁלָה עַבְדוּת תְּמוּרַת שָׁלוֹם מִלְחָמָה תְּמוּרַת חֵן כִּעוּר:

SECTION 4.

The seven double consonants are analogous to the six dimensions: height and depth, East and West, North and South, and the holy temple that stands in the centre, which carries them all.

SECTION 5.

The double consonants are seven, בגד כפרת and not six, they are seven and not eight; reflect upon this fact, inquire about it, and make it so evident, that [35] the Creator be acknowledged to be on His throne again.

SECTION 6.

The seven double consonants, stamina, having been designed and established, combined, weighed, and changed by God, He formed by them: seven planets in the world, seven days in the year, seven gates, openings of the senses, in man, male and female.

ספר יצירה

משנה ד.

שֶׁבַע כְּפוּלוֹת בְּגַ״ד כְּפָרַ״ת מַעֲלָה וּמַטָּה מִזְרָח וּמַעֲרָב צָפוֹן וְדָרוֹם וְהֵיכַל הַקּוֹדֶשׁ מְכֻוָּן בָּאֶמְצַע וְהוּא נוֹשֵׂא אֶת כֻּלָּן:

משנה ה.

שֶׁבַע כְּפוּלוֹת בְּגַ״ד כְּפָרַ״ת שִׁבְעָה וְלֹא שִׁשָּׁה שִׁבְעָה וְלֹא שְׁמוֹנָה בְּחוֹן בָּהֶם וַחֲקוֹר בָּהֶם וְהַעֲמֵד דָּבָר עַל בּוּרְיוֹ וְהוֹשֵׁב יוֹצֵר עַל מְכוֹנוֹ:

משנה ו.

שֶׁבַע כְּפוּלוֹת בְּגַ״ד כְּפָרַ״ת יְסוֹד חָקְקָן חָצְבָן צָרְפָן שְׁקָלָן וְהֵמִירָן וְצָר בָּהֶם שִׁבְעָה כוֹכָבִים בָּעוֹלָם שִׁבְעָה יָמִים בַּשָּׁנָה שִׁבְעָה שְׁעָרִים בַּנֶּפֶשׁ זָכָר וּנְקֵבָה:

SECTION 7.

The seven planets in the world are: [36] as Saturn, Jupiter, Mars, Sun, Venus, Mercury, Moon. Seven days in the year are the seven days of the week; seven gates in man, male and female, are: two eyes, two ears, two nostrils and the mouth.

SECTION 8.

FIRST DIVISION. He let the letter ב predominate in wisdom, crowned it, combined one with the other and formed by them: the moon in the world, the first day in the year, and the right eye in man, male and female.

SECTION 9.

SECOND DIVISION. He let the letter ג predominate in wealth, crowned it, combined one with the other, and formed by them: Mars in the world, the second day in the year, and the right ear in man, male and female.

ספר יצירה

משנה ז.

שִׁבְעָה כוֹכָבִים בָּעוֹלָם שַׁבְּתַי צֶדֶק מַאֲדִים חַמָּה נֹגַהּ כּוֹכָב לְבָנָה שִׁבְעָה יָמִים בְּשָׁנָה שִׁבְעָה יְמֵי הַשָּׁבוּעַ שִׁבְעָה שְׁעָרִים בְּנֶפֶשׁ זָכָר וּנְקֵבָה שְׁתֵּי עֵינַיִם שְׁתֵּי אָזְנַיִם שְׁנֵי נִקְבֵי הָאַף וְהַפֶּה:

משנה ח.

בָּבָא א. הִמְלִיךְ אוֹת בּ' בְּחָכְמָה וְקָשַׁר לוֹ כֶּתֶר וְצָרְפָן זֶה בָזֶה וְצָר בָּהֶם לְבָנָה בָּעוֹלָם יוֹם רִאשׁוֹן בְּשָׁנָה וְעַיִן יְמִין בְּנֶפֶשׁ זָכָר וּנְקֵבָה:

משנה ט.

בָּבָא ב. הִמְלִיךְ אוֹת ג' בְּעוֹשֶׁר וְקָשַׁר לוֹ כֶּתֶר וְצָרְפָן זֶה מִזֶּה וְצָר בָּהֶם מַאֲדִים בָּעוֹלָם יוֹם שֵׁנִי בְּשָׁנָה וְאֹזֶן יְמִין בְּנֶפֶשׁ זָכָר וּנְקֵבָה:

SECTION 10.

THIRD DIVISION. He let the letter ר predominate in producibility, crowned it, combined one with the other, and formed by them: the sun in the world, the third day in the year, the right nostril in man, male and female.

SECTION 11.

FOURTH DIVISION. He let the letter כ predominate in life, crowned it, combined one with the other, and formed by them: Venus in the world, the fourth day in the year, and the left eye in man, male and female.

SECTION 12.

FIFTH DIVISION. He let the letter פ predominate in dominion, crowned it, combined one with the other, and formed by them: Mercury in the world, the fifth day in the year, and the left ear in man, male and female.

ספר יצירה

משנה י.

בָּבָא ג. הִמְלִיךְ אוֹת ד׳ בִּזְרוֹעַ וְקָשַׁר לוֹ כֶּתֶר וְצָרְפָן זֶה בָזֶה וְצָר בָּהֶם חַמָּה בָּעוֹלָם יוֹם שְׁלִישִׁי בְּשָׁנָה וּנְחִיר יָמִין בְּנֶפֶשׁ זָכָר וּנְקֵבָה:

משנה י"א.

בָּא ד. הִמְלִיךְ אוֹת כ׳ בְּחַיִים וְקָשַׁר לוֹ כֶּתֶר צָרְפָן זֶה כָזֶה וְצָר בָּהֶם נוֹגַהּ בָּעוֹלָם יוֹם רְבִיעִי שָׁנָה וְאֹזֶן שְׂמֹאל בְּנֶפֶשׁ זָכָר וּנְקֵבָה:

משנה י"ב.

בָּבָא ה. הִמְלִיךְ אוֹת פ׳ בְּמֶמְשָׁלָה וְקָשַׁר לוֹ כֶּתֶר וְצָרְפָן זֶה בָזֶה וְצָר בָּהֶם כּוֹכָב בָּעוֹלָם יוֹם הַמִישִׁי בְּשָׁנָה וְאֹזֶן שְׂמֹאל בְּנֶפֶשׁ זָכָר וּנְקֵבָה:

SECTION 13.

SIXTH DIVISION. He let the letter ר predominate in peace, crowned it, combined one with the other, and formed by them: Saturn in the world, the sixth day in the year, and the left nostril in man, male and female.

SECTION 14.

SEVENTH DIVISION. He let the letter ת predominate in beauty, crowned it, combined one with the other, and formed by them: Jupiter in the world, the seventh day in the year, and the mouth of man, male and female.

ספר יצירה

משנה י"ג.

בָּבָא ו. הִמְלִיךְ אוֹת ר' בְּשָׁלוֹם וְקָשַׁר לוֹ כֶּתֶר וְצָרְפָן זֶה בָזֶה וְצָר בָּהֶם שַׁבְּתַי בָּעוֹלָם יוֹם שִׁשִּׁי בַּשָּׁנָה וּנְחִיר שְׂמֹאל בַּנֶּפֶשׁ זָכָר וּנְקֵבָה:

משנה י"ד.

בָּבָא ז. הִמְלִיךְ אוֹת תי בְּחֵן וְקָשַׁר לוֹ כֶּתֶר וְצָרְפָר זֶה בָזֶה וְצָר בָּהֶם צֶדֶק בָּעוֹלָם יוֹם שַׁבָּת בַּשָּׁנָה וּפֶה בַּנֶּפֶשׁ זָכָר וּנְקֵבָה:

SECTION 15.

By the seven double consonants, בגד כפרת were also designed seven worlds (αιωνες), seven heavens, seven lands, (probably climates,) seven seas, (probably around Palestine,) seven rivers, seven deserts, seven days a week, seven weeks from Passover to Pentecost, there is a cycle of seven years, the seventh is the release year, and after seven release years is jubilee. Hence, God loves the number seven under the whole heaven. [37] (In the whole nature.)

SECTION 16.

Two stones build two houses, three stones build six houses, four build twenty-four houses, five build one hundred and twenty houses, six build seven hundred and twenty houses and seven build five thousand and forty [38] houses. From thence further go and reckon what the mouth cannot express and the ear cannot hear.

ספר יצירה

משרה ט"ו.

שֶׁבַע בְּפוּלוֹת בְּגַ"ד כַּפְרַ"ת כַּפְרַ"ת שֶׁבְּקָקִין שִׁבְעָה

עוֹלָמוֹת שִׁבְעָה רְקִיעִין שִׁבְעָה אֲרָצוֹת שִׁבְעָה יָמִים

שִׁבְעָה נְהָרִית שִׁבְעָה מִדְבָּרוֹת שִׁבְעָה יָמִים שִׁבְעָה

שָׁבוּעוֹת שִׁבְעָה שָׁנִים שָׁבְנָה שְׁמִיטִין שִׁבְעָה יוֹבְלוֹת

לְפִיכָךְ הֲבַב אֶת הַשְּׁבִיעִיוֹת תַּחַת כָּל הַשָּׁמַיִם:

משנה ט"ז.

שְׁתֵּי אֲבָנִים בּוֹנוֹת שְׁנֵי בָתִּים שָׁלֹשׁ אֲבָנִים

בּוֹנוֹת שִׁשָּׁה בָתִּים אַרְבַּע אֲבָנִים בּוֹנוֹת אַרְבָּעָה

וְעֶשְׂרִים בָּתִּים חָמֵשׁ אֲבָנִים בּוֹנוֹת מֵאָה וְעֶשְׂרִים

בָּתִּים שֵׁשׁ אֲבָנִים בּוֹנוֹת שְׁבַע מֵאוֹת וְעֶשְׂרִים

בָּתִּים שֶׁבַע אֲבָנִים בּוֹנוֹת חֲמֵשֶׁת אֲלָפִים

(וארבע) וְאַרְבָּעִים בָּתִּים מִכָּאן וְאֵילָךְ צֵא וַחֲשׁוֹב

מַה שֶּׁאֵין הַפֶּה יְכוֹלָה לְדַבֵּר וְאֵין הָאֹזֶן יְכוֹלָה

לִשְׁמוֹעַ:

CHAPTER V.

SECTION 1.

The twelve simple letters עצק-לבס-תטי-הוז symbolize, as it were, the organs of speaking, thinking, [36] walking, seeing, hearing, working, coition, smelling, sleep, anger, swallowing and laughing.

SECTION 2.

The twelve simple consonants עצק-לבס-תטי-הוז symbolize also twelve oblique points: east height, north east, east depth, south height, south east, south depth, west height, south west, west depth, north height, north west, north depth. They grew wider and wider to all eternity, and these are the boundaries of the world.

ספר יצירה
פרק חמישי.

משנה א.

שְׁתֵּים עֶשְׂרֵה פְּשׁוּטוֹת הו״ז חט״י לנ״ם עצ״ק

יְסוֹדָן שִׂיחָה הִרְהוּר הִלּוּךְ רְאִיָה שְׁמִיעָה מַעֲשֶׂה

תַּשְׁמִישׁ רֵיחַ שֵׁינָה רוֹגֶז לְעִיטָה שְׂחוֹק:

משנה ב.

שְׁתֵּים עֶשְׂרֵה פְּשׁוּטוֹת הו״ז חט״י לנ״ם עצ״ק

יְסוֹדָן שְׁנֵים עָשָׂר גְּבוּלֵי אֲלַכְסוֹן גְּבוּל מִזְרָחִית

רוֹמִית גְּבוּל מִזְרָחִית צְפוֹנִית גְּבוּל מִזְרָחִית תַּחְתִּית

גְּבוּל דְּרוֹמִית רוֹמִית גְּבוּל דְּרוֹמִית יְמִזְרָחִית גְּבוּל

דְּרוֹמִית תַּחְתִּית גְּבוּל מַעֲרָבִית רוֹמִית גְּבוּל

מַעֲרָבִית דְּרוֹמִית גְּבוּל מַעֲרָבִית תַּחְתִּית גְּבוּל

צְפוֹנִית רוֹמִית גְּבוּל צְפוֹנִית מַעֲרָבִית גְּבוּל צְפוֹנִית

תַּחְתִּית וּמִתְרַחֲבִין וְהֵי לְכִין עַד עֲדֵי עַד וְהֵן הֵן

גְּבוּלוֹת עוֹלָם:

SECTION 3.

The twelve simple letters הוז-תטי-לבס-עצק stamina, having been designed, established, combined, weighed and changed by God, He performed by them: twelve constellations in the world, twelve months in the year, and twelve leaders (organs) in the human body, male and female.

SECTION 4.

The twelve constellations in the world are: Aries, Taurus, Gemini, Cancer, Leo, Virgo, Libra, Scorpio, Sagitarius, Capricornus, Aquarius and Pisces. The twelve months of the year are: Nisan, Iyar, Sivan, Tamus, Ab, Elul, Tishri, Marcheshvan, Kislev, Teves, Schevat and Adar. The twelve organs of the human body are: two hands, two feet, two kidneys, gall, small intestines, liver, gullet or esophagus, stomach and milt.

ספר יצירה
משנה ג.

שְׁתֵּים עֶשְׂרֵה פְּשׁוּטוֹת הו״ז חט״י לנ״י עצ״ק יְסוֹדָן הַקַּקֵן הַצְּבָן הַצְּבָן צָרְפָן שָׁקְלָן וְהֵמִירָן וְצָר בָּהֶם שְׁתֵּים עֶשְׂרֵה מַזָּלוֹת בָּעוֹלָם שְׁנֵים עָשָׂר חֳדָשִׁים בְּשָׁנָה שְׁנֵים עָשָׂר מַנְהִיגִים בַּנֶּפֶשׁ זָכָר וּנְקֵבָה:

משנה ד.

שְׁתֵּים עֶשְׂרֵה מַזָּלוֹת בָּעוֹלָם טָלֶה שׁוֹר תְּאוֹמִים סַרְטָן אַרְיֵה בְּתוּלָה מ׳ אזְנַיִם עַקְרָב קֶשֶׁת גְּדִי דְּלִי דָּגִים: שְׁנֵים עָשָׂר חֳדָשִׁים בְּשָׁנָה נִיסָן אִיָּיר סִיוָן תַּמּוּז אָב אֱלוּל תִּשְׁרֵי חֶשְׁוָן כִּסְלֵו טֵבֵת שְׁבָט אֲדָר: שְׁנֵים עָשָׂר מַנְהִיגִים בַּנֶּפֶשׁ זָכָר וּנְקֵבָה שְׁתֵּי יָדַיִם שְׁתֵּי רַגְלַיִם שְׁתֵּי כְּלָיוֹת מָרָה דַּקִּין כָּבֵד (קורקבן) גַּרְגֶּרֶת קֵבָה טְחוֹל:

SECTION 5.

First Part.

FIRST DIVISION. God let the letter ה predominate in speaking, crowned it, combined one with the other, and formed by them: Aries (the Ram) in the world, the month Nisan in the year, and the right foot of the human body, male and female.

SECTION 6.

SECOND DIVISION. He let the letter ו predominate in thinking, crowned it, combined one with the other, and formed by them: Taurus (the Bull) in the world, the month Iyar in the year and the right kidney of the human body, male and female.

SECTION 7.

THIRD DIVISION. He let the letter ז predominate in walking, crowned it, combined one with the other, and formed by them: Gemini (the Twins) in the world, the month Sivan in the year, and the left foot of the human body, male and female.

ספר יצירה
משנה ה.

בָּבָא א׳ מֵהָא. הִמְלִיךְ אוֹת ה׳ בְּשִׂיחָה וְקָשַׁר לוֹ כֶּתֶר וְצָרְפָן זֶה בָזֶה וְצָר בָּהֶם טָלֶה בָּעוֹלָם וְכִיסָן בְּשָׁנָה וְרֶגֶל יָמִין בְּנֶפֶשׁ זָכָר וּנְקֵבָה:

משנה ו.

בָּבָא ב׳ מֵהָא. הִמְלִיךְ אוֹת י׳ בְּהִרְהוּר וְקָשַׁר לוֹ כֶּתֶר וְצָרְפָן זֶה בָזֶה וְצָר בָּהֶם שׁוֹר בָּעוֹלָם וְאִיָּיר בְּשָׁנָה וְכוּלְיָא יְמָנִית בְּנֶפֶשׁ זָכָר וּנְקֵבָה:

משנה ז.

בָּבָא ג׳ מֵהָא. הִמְלִיךְ אוֹת ז׳ בְּהִלּוּךְ וְקָשַׁר לוֹ כֶּתֶר וְצָרְפָן זֶה בָזֶה וְצָר בָּהֶם בְּאוֹמִים בָּעוֹלָם וְסִיוָן בְּשָׁנָה וְרֶגֶל שָׂם אֵל בְּנֶפֶשׁ זָכָר וּנְקֵבָה:

SECTION 8.

Second Part.

FIRST DIVISION. He let the letter ח predominate in seeing, crowned it, combined one with the other, and formed by them: Cancer (the Crab) in the world, the month Tamus in the year, and the right hand of the human body, male and female.

SECTION 9.

SECOND DIVISION. He let the letter ט predominate in hearing, crowned it, combined one with the other, and formed by them: Leo (the Lion) in the world, the month Ab in the year, and the left kidney of the human body, male and female.

SECTION 10.

THIRD DIVISION. He let the letter י predominate in working, crowned it, combined one with the other, and formed by them: Virgo (the Virgin) in the world, the month Elul in the year, and the left hand of the human body, male and female.

ספר יצירה

משנה ח.

בָּבָא א׳ מִן הַשְּׁנִיָּה. הִמְלִיךְ אוֹת חי בִּרְאִיָּה וְקָשַׁר לוֹ כֶּתֶר וְצָרְפָן זֶה בָּזֶה וְצָר בָּהֶם סַרְטָן בָּעוֹלָם וְתַמּוּז בְּשָׁנָה וְיַד יָמִין בְּנֶפֶשׁ זָכָר וּנְקֵבָה:

משנה ט.

בָּבָא ב׳ מִן הַשְּׁנִיָּה. הִמְלִיךְ אוֹת ט׳ בְּשַׁמֵּי עָה וְקָשַׁר לוֹ כֶּתֶר וְצָרְפָן זֶה בָּזֶה וְצָר בָּהֶם אַרְיֵה בָּעוֹלָם וְאָב בְּשָׁנָה וְכוּלְיָא שְׂמָאלִית בְּנֶפֶשׁ זָכָר וּנְקֵבָה:

משנה י.

בָּבָא ג׳ מִן הַשְּׁנִיָּה. הִמְלִיךְ אוֹת י׳ בְּמַעֲשֶׂה וְקָשַׁר לוֹ כֶּתֶר וְצָרְפָן זֶה בָּזֶה וְצָר בָּהֶם בְּתוּלָה בָּעוֹלָם וֶאֱלוּל בְּשָׁנָה וְיַד שְׂמֹ אל בְּנֶפֶשׁ זָכָר וּנְקֵבָה:

SECTION 11.

Third Part.

FIRST DIVISION. He let the letter ל predominate in coition, crowned it, combined one with the other, and formed by them: Libra (the Balance) in the world, the month Tishri in the year, and the gall of the human body, male and female.

SECTION 12.

SECOND DIVISION. He let the letter נ predominate in smelling, crowned it, combined one with the other, and formed by them: Scorpio (the Scorpion) in the world, the month Marcheshvan in the year, and the small intestines of the human body, male and female.

SECTION 13.

THIRD DIVISION. He let the letter ס predominate in sleep, crowned it, combined one with the other, and formed by them: Sagittarius (the Archer) in the world, the month Kislev in the year, and the stomach of the human body, male and female.

ספר יצירה

משנה י"א.

בָּבָא א׳ מִן הַשְּׁלִישִׁית. הִמְלִיךְ אוֹת ל׳ בְּתַשְׁמִישׁ וְקָשַׁר לוֹ כֶּתֶר וְצָרְפָן זֶה בָזֶה וְצָר בָּהֶם מֹ אזְנַיִם בְּעוֹלָם וְתִשְׁרֵי בְּשָׁנָה וּמָרָה בְּנֶפֶשׁ זָכָר וּנְקֵבָה:

משנה י"ב.

בָּבָא ב׳ מִן הַשְּׁלִישִׁית. הִמְלִיךְ אוֹת נ׳ בְּרֵיחַ וְקָשַׁר לוֹ כֶּתֶר וְצָרְפָן זֶה בָזֶה וְצָר בָּהֶם עַקְרָב בְּעוֹלָם וּמַרְחֶשְׁוָן בְּשָׁנָה וְדַקִין בְּנֶפֶשׁ זָכָר וּנְקֵבָה:

משנה י"ג.

בָּבָא ג׳ מִן הַשְּׁלִישִׁית. הִמְלִיךְ אוֹת ס׳ בְּשֵׁנָה וְקָשַׁר לוֹ כֶּתֶר וְצָרְפָן זֶה בָזֶה וְצָר בָּהֶם גְּדִי בְּעוֹלָם טֵבֵת בְּשָׁנָה וְכָבֵד בְּנֶפֶשׁ זָכָר וּנְקֵבָה:

Sepher Yetzirah   Book of Creation

SECTION 14.

Fourth Part.

FIRST DIVISION. He let the letter ע predominate in anger, crowned it, combined one with the other, and formed by them: Capricornus (the Goat) in the world, the month Teves in the year, and the liver in the human body, male and female.

SECTION 15.

SECOND DIVISION. He let the letter צ predominate in swallowing, crowned it, combined one with the other, and formed by them: Aquarius (the Water-man) in the world, the month Schwat in the year, and the esophagus of the human body, male and female.

SECTION 16.

THIRD DIVISION. He let the letter ק predominate in laughing, crowned it, combined one with the other, and formed by them: Pisces (the Fishes) in the world, the month Adar in the year, and the milt of the human body, male and female. He made them as a conflict, drew them up like a wall; and set one against the other as in warfare.

ספר יצירה

מִשְׁנָה י״ד.

בָּבָה א׳ מִן הָרְבִיעִית. הִמְלִיךְ אוֹת ע׳ בְּרוֹגֶז

וְקָשַׁר לוֹ כֶּתֶר וְצָרְפָן זֶה בָּהּ וְצָר בָּהֶם גְּדִי בָּעוֹלָם

טֵבֵת בַּשָּׁנָה וְכָבֵד בַּנֶּפֶשׁ זָכָר וּנְקֵבָה:

מִשְׁנָה ט״ו.

בָּבָא ב׳ מִן הָרְבִיעִית. הִמְלִיךְ אוֹת צ׳ בִּלְעִיטָה

וְקָשַׁר לוֹ כֶּתֶר וְצָרְפָן זֶה בְּזֶה בָּהֶם דְּלִי בָּעוֹלָם

וּשְׁבָט בַּשָּׁנָה (נקורקבן) וְגַרְגֶּרֶת בַּנֶּפֶשׁ זָכָר וּנְקֵבָה:

מִשְׁנָה ט״ז.

בָּבָא ג׳ מִן הָרְבִיעִית. הִמְלִיךְ אוֹת ק׳ בִּשְׂחוֹק

וְקָשַׁר לוֹ כֶּתֶר וְצָרְפָן זֶה בְּזֶה וְצָר בָּהֶם דָּגִים בַּצּוּלָם

וַאֲדָר בַּשָּׁנָה וּטְחוֹל בַּנֶּפֶשׁ זָכָר וּבִקְבָה עָשָׂאָן כְּמִין

עֲרִיבָה* סִידְרָן כְּמִין חוֹמָה עָרְכָן כְּמִין מִלְחָמָה:

*) נ״א מְרִיבָה אוֹ מְרִינָה:

CHAPTER VI.

SECTION 1.

These are the three mothers or the first elements, אמש from which emanated three progenitors; primitive air, water and fire, and from which emanated as their offspring, three progenitors and their offspring, namely: the seven planets and their hosts, and the twelve oblique points.

SECTION 2.

To confirm this there are faithful witnesses; the world, year and man, the twelve, the Equipoise, the heptade, which God regulates like the Dragon, [40] (Tali) sphere and the heart.

SECTION 3.

The first elements אמש are air, water and fire; the fire is above, the water below, and a breath of air establishes the balance among them. For an illustration may serve, that the fire carries the water is the phonetic character of מ which is mute and ש is hissing like fire, there is א among them, a breath of air which places them in equilibrium. [41]

ספר יצירה
פרק ששי.

משנה א.

עֵלוּ הֵם שָׁלֹשׁ אִמּוֹת אֱמֶ״שׁ וְיָצְאוּ מֵהֶם שְׁלֹשָׁה

אָבוֹת וְהֵם אֲוִיר וּמַיִם וָאֵשׁ וּמֵאָבוֹת תּוֹלְדוֹת שְׁלֹשָׁה

אָבוֹת וְתוֹלְדוֹתֵיהֶם וְשִׁבְעָה כּוֹכָבִים וְצִבְאוֹתֵיהֶם

וּשְׁנֵים עָשָׂר גְּבוּלֵי אֲלַכְסוֹן:

משנה ב.
רְאָיָה לַדָּבָר עֵדִים נֶאֱמָנִים בָּעוֹלָם שָׁנָה נֶפֶשׁ

וּשְׁנֵים עָשָׂר חָק וְשִׁבְעָה וּשְׁלֹשָׁה וּפְקָדָן כְּתֵלִי

וְגַלְגַּל וָלֵב:

משנה ג.
שָׁלֹשׁ אִמּוֹת אֱמֶ״שׁ אֲוִיר אֵשׁ וּמַיִם אֵשׁ לְמַעְלָה

וּמַיִם לְמַטָּה וְאֲוִיר רוּחַ חָק מַכְרִיעַ בֵּנְתַיִם וְסִימָן

לַדָּבָר הָאֵשׁ נוֹשֵׂא אֶת הַמַּיִם מִ״י דוֹמֶמֶת שִׁי שׁוֹרֶקֶת

אִ י אֲוִיר רוּחַ חָק מַכְרִיעַ בֵּנְתַיִם:

SECTION 4.

Dragon (Tali) is in the world like a king upon his throne, the sphere is in the year like a king in the empire, and the heart is in the human body like a king [42] in war.

SECTION 5.

God has also set the one over against the other; the good against the evil, and the evil against the good; the good proceeds from the good, and the evil from the evil; the good purifies the bad, and the bad the good; the good is preserved for the good, and the evil for the bad ones.

SECTION 6.

There are three of which every one of them stands by itself; one is in the affirmative, the other in the negative and one equalizes them.

ספר יצירה

משנה ד.
תְּלִי בָּעוֹלָם כְּמֶלֶךְ עַל כִּסְאוֹ גַּלְגַּל בְּשָׁנָה כְּמֶלֶךְ בִּמְדִינָה* לֵב בַּנֶּפֶשׁ כְּמֶלֶךְ בְּמִלְחָמָה:

*) נייא על חומה:

משנה ה.
גַּם אֶת זֶה לְעֻמַּת זֶה עָשָׂה אֱלֹהִים טוֹב לְעֻמַּת רָע רָע לְעֻמַּת טוֹב טוֹב מִטּוֹב רָע מֵרָע הַטּוֹב מַבְחִין אֶת הָרַע וְהָרַע מַבְחִין אֶת הַטּוֹב טוֹבָה שְׁמוּרָה לַטּוֹבִים וְרָעָה שְׁמוּרָה לָרָעִים:

משנה ו.
שְׁלֹשָׁה כָּל אֶחָד לְבַדּוֹ עוֹמֵד אֶחָד מְזַכֶּה וְאֶחָד מְחַיֵּיב וְאֶחָד מַכְרִיעַ בֵּנְתַיִם:

SECTION 7.

There are seven of which three are against three, and one places them in equilibrium. There are twelve which are all the time at war; three of them produce love, and three hatred, three are animators and three destroyers.

SECTION 8.

The three that produce love are the heart and the ears; the three that produce hatred are the liver, the gall and the tongue; the three animators are the two nostrils and the milt; and the three destroyers are the mouth and the two openings of the body; and God, the faithful King, rules over all from His holy habitation to all eternity. He is one above three, three are above seven, seven above twelve, and all are linked together.

ספר יצירה

משנה ז.

שִׁבְעָה שְׁלֹשָׁה מוּל שְׁלֹשָׁה וְאֶחָד מַכְרִיעַ בְּנָתַיִם וּשְׁנֵים עָשָׂר עוֹמְדִין בַּמִּלְחָמָה: שְׁלֹשָׁה אוֹהֲבִים שְׁלֹשָׁה שׂוֹנְאִים שְׁלֹשָׁה מְחַיִּים וּשְׁלֹשָׁה מְמִיתִים:

משנה ח.

שְׁלֹשָׁה אוֹהֲבִים הַלֵּב וְהָאָזְנַיִם שְׁלֹשָׁה שׂוֹנְאִים הַכָּבֵד הַמָּרָה וְהַלָּשׁוֹן שְׁלֹשָׁה מְחַיִּים שְׁנֵי נִקְבֵי הָאַף וְהַטְּחוֹל ושלשה ממיתים שני הנקבים והפה ואל מלך נאמן מושל בכלם ממעון קדשו עד עדי עד אחד על גבי שלשה שלשה על גבי שבעה שבעה על גבי שנים עשר וכלם אדוקים זה בזה:

SECTION 9.

There [43] are twenty-two letters by which the I am, Yah, the Lord of hosts, Almighty and Eternal, designed, formed and created by three Sepharim, His whole world, and formed by them creatures and all those that will be formed in time to come.

SECTION 10.

When [44] the patriarch Abraham comprehended the great truism, revolved it in his mind, conceived it perfectly, made careful investigations and profound inquiries, pondered upon it and succeeded in contemplations, the Lord of the Universe appeared to him, called him his friend, made with him a covenant between the ten fingers of his hands, which is the covenant of the tongue, [45] and the covenant between the ten toes of his feet, which is the covenant of circumcision, and said of him: "Before I formed thee in the belly I knew thee." (Jer. I, 5.)

ספר יצירה

משנה ט.

או הֵם עֶשְׂרִים וּשְׁתַּיִם אוֹתִיּוֹת שֶׁבָּהֶן חָקַק אֶהְיֶה יָהּ יְהוָ"ה צְבָאוֹת אֵל שַׁדַּי יְהוָ"ה אֱלֹהִ"ים וְעָשָׂה מֵהֶם שְׁלֹשָׁה סְפָרִים וּבָרָא מֵהֶם אֶת כָּל עוֹלָמוֹ וְצָר בָּהֶם אֶת כָּל הַיְצוּר וְאֶת כָּל הֶעָתִיד לָצוּר:

משנה י.

וּכְשֶׁהֵבִין אַבְרָהָם אָבִינוּ וְהִבִּיט וְרָאָה וְחָקַק וְחָצַב וְעָלְתָה בְיָדוֹ נִגְלָה עָלָיו אֲדוֹן הַכֹּ"ל וּקְרָאוֹ אוֹהֲבִי וְכָרַת לוֹ בְּרִית בֵּין עֶשֶׂר אֶצְבְּעוֹת יָ"ד דָּיוֹ וְהוּא בְּרִית הַלָּשׁוֹן וּבֵין עֶשֶׂר אֶצְבְּעוֹת רַגְלָיו וְהוּא בְּרִית הַמִּילָה וְקָרָא עָלָיו בְּטֶרֶם אֶצָּרְךָ בַבֶּטֶן יְדַעְתִּיךָ:*

*) נ"א וקשר עשרים ושתים אותיו ת בלשונו ונלה לו את יסונץ משכנו במים דלקן כאש רעשו ברות בערן בשבעה נהנן בשתים עשרת מולות:

סליק פרקא. וסליק ספר יצירה:

Sepher Yetzirah   *Book of Creation*

NOTES.

[1] Our author maintains that there is a first intelligent, self-existing, almighty, eternal ruling cause of all things, and that an everlasting entity produced nonentities by a progression of effects. The divine knowledge, he adds, differs from the human knowledge in such a degree, that it gives existence to all that is. חפפ יח ח"י צבאות is a talmudical expression. (See Treatise Bava Bathra p. 93.) It seems to me, that the author not only wanted to contradict Plato's assertion that the Supreme Being had need of a plan, like the human architect, to conduct the great design, when he made the fabric of the Universe, but also the common belief that God reasons and acts by ideas like a human being. As the prophet Isaiah exclaimed: "Behold! God has no ideas like you, and his ways of acting are not like yours." (Isaiah 55, 8-9.)

[2] The number thirty-two is not only the fifth power of two, and the sum of ten units and twenty-two letters, but is also the sum of the first and last letter of the Hebrew Pentateuch, namely: ב 2 and 30, equal thirty-two. (See Kusari p. 343, translated into German by Dr. David Cassel.)

[3] Paths denote powers, effects, kinds, forms, degrees or stages.

[4] These Sepharim or three words of similar expression signify: first, number, calculation or idea; second, the word; third, the writing of the *word. The idea, word and writing (of the word), are signs to man for a thing, and is not the thing itself, to the Creator, however,

ספר יצירה

idea, word and writing (of the word) are the thing itself, or as some ancient Rabbis remarked: "מחשבה דביר ומעשה הכל הרא דבו אחד בהקי"ב"יהי", Idea, word and work are one and the same to God." There is an ideal world in the divine intellect, according to which this sensible world was made. The difference between the human and divine manner of thinking admits no comparison.

⁵ This means to say, that there has not been any matter or hyle existing from all eternity, containing different kinds of primitive atoms or molecules etc., as the Greek philosopher, Anaxagoras, taught, but that all things are the gradual emanations of one everlasting being. This idea is then symbolically explained in the next paragraph.

⁶ The design of the author is evidently to deduce the proof of the decade from the phenomena in the nature of man, who is generally considered the crown or the final cause of the terrestrial creation, and upon whom God vouchsafed two most precious gifts, namely: the articulated word, and the religious element (spiritual purity). This passage is explained by Isaac Satanow in his Hebrew Dictionary entitled Sephath Emeth, p. 44, b:

דחנח הלשין הוא עט סופר לתולדות חשכלים ואבר המוליד

לתולדות החמריים ובל אחד הוא ברית עולם לקיים את האדם

לפליטה נצחרת על שתי צלעותיו חמרו וצורתו האי כדאיתיח

והאי כדאיתיה זה בחמרו וזה בצורתו.

The tongue is, as it were, the descriptive pen of all the spiritual issues, and the genital parts are the originators of the corporeal substances. Every one of them is an eternal covenant in order to preserve the human race for ever, according to its two-fold being: body and spirit. Each working after its own way, physically and spiritually.

[7]) Like Pythagoras, who taught that the digits inclusive number ten which are typified in Tetraktys, (Τετρακτυς) namely: 1 plus 2 plus 3 plus 4 equal 10, and which comprise the whole arithmetical system of nature, etc. Our author endeavors to show the gradual emanation of all things from God, which were completely finished in ten spheres.

[8] My Hebrew reading is: חושב יוצר על There are various readings; therefore Postellus rendered it: "restitue figmentum in locum suum;" Rittangel, "restitue formatorem in throno suo;" Pistorius, "fac sedere creatorem in throno suo." The author seems to ridicule here the Gnosticians who maintained that Demiurg was the creator of man and the sensual world.

[9] In God is the beginning and he is the boundary of the Universe. Compare also the Talmud treatise Chagigah p. 12.

[10] Here is contradicted the system of ditheism, consisting of an eternal God, the Author of all good and of "Hyle" or "Satan," the co-eternal and co-equal principle of evil, maintaining that an all-perfect God alone is the author of all good and evil, and has in his

ספר יצירה

infinite wisdom so wonderfully contrived the nature of things, that physical and moral evil may produce good, and hence contribute to carry out the great design of the Supreme Being. Compare also Chap. 6 §5.

[11] As the infinite series of numbers starts from one unit, so was the whole Universe formed a unity, that centres in the Godhead.

[12] The meaning is, that as the living creatures which the prophet saw in his vision were stricken with such an awe, that they could not go any further to see the divine glory, and had to return, so is the decade an eternal secret to us and we are not permitted to understand it. We find this very idea in the Pythagorean system. The disciples of Pythagoras looked upon the decade as a holy number, and swore by it and by the Tetraktys which contain the number ten,

[13] See above Note 1, God, idea and word are indivisible.

[14] I adopted here the reading of Judah Halevi, namely:

חקק וחצב בהו

בהו רפש וטיט וגו׳,

with the exception of the word תהו because it is obvious from "Yezirah," Chap. II, that the author signifies by the word "Tohu," nothing, and not something, as Judah Halevi erroneously thought.

Moses Butarel and others tell us that they had before them a correct copy of "Sepher Yezirah," where it reads:

תהו זה קו ירוק וכו' בהו אלו אבנים

מפולמות:

The same passage is mentioned in the Talmud treatise Chagigah, p. 12, a, with the addition of

המשוקעות בתהום שמהן יוצאין

מים.

The word מפולמות, is translated by Rashi, *moist*. Some say it is a compound word of מפול מות, others of פלוני אלמוני, etc. But the word is not of Semitic origin; it is, according to my opinion, borrowed from the Greek as the word סימו etc., ח πλημυν *flood*. אבנים מפלמות flood-stones. The same word is used treatise Beza, p. 24, b, המפולמין fish that are caught from out of the flood.

[15] According to the author, the space and six dimensions emanated from the ether.

[16] Judah Halevi in his book entitled "Kusari," p. 456, illustrates it thus: The Creator is one, and the space has in the figurative

ספר יצירה

expression six dimensions. The book "Yezirah," having ascribed to the Creator some names in the spiritual language, chooses now in the human language the finest sounds which are, as it were, the spirits of the other sounds, namely: "הוי" and says, that when the divine will was expressed by such a sublime name, it became that which the Exalted by praise wished to call forth according to the combination of "הוי." Hence it follows, that the material world was created in such a way and manner which corresponds with the material, namely, by the sublime spiritual name, which corresponds with the material name, והי, ויה, היו, הוי, ויה, יהו, and out of each of them became one dimension of the world, the sphere.

[17] The author shows here by the symbol of a scale and the phonetic character of the fundamental letters, א-מ-ש that the opposite forces and the struggle which prevail in the smallest as well as in the largest circles of creation are appeased and calmed.

[18] Meaning outlets, outgates of the creative power, formations.

[19] The word ענג signifies joy, and when transposed, forming the word נגע it signifies just the contrary, trouble, plague. He means to say, that the letters of the words ענג and נגע are the same, but they signify nevertheless, opposite ideas on account of transposition. Just as the sphere remains the same during the rotation on its axis in its setting and in its rising; yet it appears to us as if it had undergone a great change on account of its different position.

Sepher Yetzirah   Book of Creation

[20] My reading is עָרְכָּו שָׁקְלוּ וְחַמִיָּו.

[21] The combination of the twenty-two letters without permutation is represented in the following table:

אב אג אד אה או אז אח אט אי אכ אל אם אן אס אע אפ אצ אק אר אש את
בג בד בה בו בז בח בט בי בכ בל בם בן בס בע בף בץ בק בר בש בת
גד גה גו גז גח גט גי גכ גל גם גן גס גע גף גץ גק גר גש גת
דה דו דז דח דט די דכ דל דם דן דס דע דף דץ דק דר דש דת
הו הז הח הט הי הכ הל הם הן הס הע הף הץ הק הר הש הת
וז וח וט וי וכ ול ום ון וס וע וף וץ וק ור וש ות
זח זט זי זכ זל זם זן זס זע זף זץ זק זר זש זת
חט חי חכ חל חם חן חס חע חף חץ חק חר חש חת
טי טכ טל טם טן טס טע טף טץ טק טר טש טת
יכ יל ים ין יס יע יף יץ יק יר יש ית
כל כם כן כס כע כף כץ כק כר כש כת
לם לן לס לע לף לץ לק לר לש לת
מן מס מע מף מץ מק מר מש מת
נס נע נף נץ נק נר נש נת
סע סף סץ סק סר סש סת
עף עץ עק ער עש עת
פץ פק פר פש פת
צק צר צש צת
קר קש קת
רש רת
שת

[22]) The number of combinations of twenty-two letters two and two without any permutation is according to the mathematical formula

ספר יצירה

$$\frac{n-1}{2} = \frac{22-1}{2} = 22-1 \times \frac{22}{2} = 231.$$

²³ The ancient philosophers maintained that if God is the first cause, and He is necessarily, He, the immediate effect of Him, as an absolute unity, can only be again a unity. Hence from a being that is in every respect a unique being, there can only emanate one being; because would two essentially and truly different things issue conjointly from one being, they can only proceed from two different things of substance, that would consequently admit a division that is inconceivable. They then put the question, how came so many various beings into existence? Our author is therefore endeavoring to show that the whole universe emanated gradually from the spirit of the one living God.

²⁴ The reading of Von Jo. Meyer and others is as follows:

יצר מתוחו

ממש ועשה אינו ישנו והצב עמודים גדולים מאויר שאינו נתפס

ויח סימן צופח ומימר עושח כל היצור ואת כל הדברים בשם אחר

וסימן לדבר עשרים ושתים מניינם דגוף אחג:

My reading according to a manuscript of Rabbi Isaac Luria, which I have preferred to all others, is thus:

Sepher Yetzirah   *Book of Creation*

יצר ממש מתוהו ועשה את אינו ישנו וחצב עמודים גדולים

מאדיר שאינו נתפס וזה סימן אות א עם כולן וכולן עם א צופה

ומימר ועשה את כל היצור ואת כל חדבור שם אחד וסימן לדבר

עשרום ושתים חפצים בגוף א׃

[25] It has been already mentioned above Chap. i, §1, that God, his idea and his word are a unity; hence the author signifies by the letter Aleph the air from which emanated the creative speech, etc.

[26] Here is meant: ethereal air, ethereal water, ethereal fire, the macrocosm, the courses of time and microcosm. Many offspring or derivations came from the latter three, as their progenitors, as it is explained afterwards in the chapter.

[27] The author endeavors to show how the creative divine word became more condensed and how a new series of productions came out of three elements.

[28] In ancient times coldness was considered to be a substance. [See Psalm 147, 17.]

[29] Id est, made it the reigning power.

[30] Namely, with the two other elements.

[31] That is to say a different combination of the elements.

ספר יצירה

[32] According to the opinion of the author, it may be arranged as follows:

	א Aleph.	מ Mem.	ש Sheen.
World:	Air,	Earth, (Inclusive of Land and Sea)	Heaven or Atmosphere.
Man:	Breast,	Belly,	Head.
Year:	Moistness,	Coldness, Heat.	

[33] The aspirating pronunciation of Ρ in the Greek, was adopted by the ancient Jews in Palestine for the Hebrew letter ר. They pronounced it partly aspirated and partly unaspirated. [See Dr. Geiger's Lehr-und Lese-buch der Mischnah, p. 22, and Dr. Graetz's Gnosticismus, p. 117.]

[34] According to the idea of our author, there emanated from the unity of God three ethereal elements: primitive air from the spirit, from the air, primitive water, and from the water, primitive fire or ether, out of which came other spheres of existence in the significant and highly important number, seven, from which descended smaller spheres and which produced again others. He endeavors to show how the ideal became, after numerous emanations, more condensed, palpable and concrete. The whole creation is thus contemplated as a pyramid, terminating in a point at the top with a broad basis. [See Dr. Graetz's Gnosticismus, p. 224.]

[35] Compare Chapter I, Section 3, Note, 8.

³⁶ The order of the planets (including the Sun) is stated here according to the Ptolemaic system which was in vogue even among the learned men till the middle of the fifteenth century, namely: Moon, Mercury, Venus, Sun, Mars, Jupiter and Saturn. But this arrangement is undoubtedly an interpolation of a later time, as the author of the book "Yezirah" lived many years before Ptolemy. And indeed Prof. Jo. Friedrich Von Meyer and others of reliable authority had in their copies of "Yezirah" the following order: חמה נוגה כוכב לבנה שבתי צדק מאדים. Mars, Jupiter, Saturn, Moon, Mercury, Venus, Sun.

³⁷ Philo (Allegor 1, 42,) after having called attention to the fact that the heptade is to be found in many biblical laws, in the vowels of the Greek language, in the gamut and in the organs of the human body, exclaims, similar to our author: "The whole nature exults in the heptade!"

³⁸ The rule for permutation is as follows: (n--1) n. 1 x 2 x 3 x 4 x 5 x 6 x 7=5040. In our edition it reads: בתים חמשת אלפים חמשת ארבע Five thousand and four houses, which is obviously a mistake, it should read: 5040 houses. וארבעם בתים אלפים

³⁹ I read גרגרת instead of קורקובן for two reasons. In the first place, the same thing is mentioned afterwards, and in the second place, it is proved by the expression לעיטה that the author meant גרגרת and not קורקובן.

ספר יצירה

[40] Some maintain that by the expression Tali is understood the constellation Draco or Dragon, which is a very large constellation extending for a great length from East to West; beginning at the tail which lies half way between the Pointers and the Pole Star, and winding round between the Great and Little Bear by a continued succession of bright stars from 5 to 10 degrees asunder, it coils round under the feet of the Little Bear, sweeps round the pole of the ecliptic, and terminates in a trapezium formed by four conspicuous stars from 30 to 35 degrees from North Pole. Dr. Steinshneider (see Magazin fuer Literatur des Auslandes, 1845) and Dr. Cassel (in his commentary to the book entitled Kusari,) maintain that the ancient Jewish astronomers signified by the word Tali, not the constellation Draco, but the line which joins together the two points in which the orbit of the moon intercepts the ecliptic (Dragon's head and tail). Dr. Cassel is of the opinion that our author meant here, probably the invisible, celestial or universal axis that carries the whole Universe.

[41] Our author means to say that the water has a great disposition to unite itself with the caloric, thus for instance is the fire latent in steam, but the air equipoises them.

[42] The meaning is, as God is the centre of the Universe, so have the macrocosm, the seasons and temperature and the microcosm, their centres receiving power from the principal centre to regulate and rule.

[43] The substance of this Mishnah is mentioned in the Talmud treatise Berachoth, p. 55, a. It reads there:

Sepher Yetzirah — Book of Creation

אמר רב יהידה אמר רב יודע היה

בצלעל לצרף אותיות שנבראו בהן שמים וארץ:

"Rab Jehudah stated in the name of Rab, that Bezalel understood to combine letters by which heaven and earth were created." To this the commentator Rashi adds: "as it is taught in the book Yezirah." It is undoubtedly certain that the book Yezirah, or a cosmogony as it is represented there, was known to Rab, who was a disciple of Jehudah Hanasi, during the second part of the second century. (C. E.) See treatise Berachoth, p. 55 a, where the commentator Rashi referred to the book Yezirah.

[44] This whole paragraph is an interpolation of an unknown hand, as it can be easily proved.

[45] I have translated according to the reading of Rabbi Judah Halevi. The reading of Rabbi Luria is as follows:

וקשר עשרים ושתים אותיות

בלשונו וגילח לו את סודו משכן במים דלקן באש רעשן בויח בערן

בשבעה נהגין בשנים עשר

"He fastened twenty-two letters on his tongue and revealed to him His mystery, He drew them by water, kindled them by fire and thundered them by the wind, He lighted them by seven, and rules them by twelve constellations." Pistor. renders it: "Tranat per

ספר יצירה

aquam, accendit in igne grandine signavit in äere. Disposuit cum septem et gubernavit cum duodecim." Postellus' version is: "Attraxit eam in aqua, accendit in spiritu, inflammavit in septem aptatum cum duodecim signis." Meyer translates it: "Er zog sie mit Wasser, zündet sie an mit Feuer, erregte sie mit Geist, vebrannte sie mit sieben, goes sie aus mit den swoelf Gestirnen."

Sepher Yetzirah — *Book of Creation*

GLOSSARY OF RABBINICAL WORDS.

א

אָדַק *v.* To adhere, cohere. VI, 8.

אַדָּר *n.* [Syriac אאר, Greek αηρ] Air. II.

אוֹת *n.* Sign, letter; אוֹתִיוֹת יְסוֹד fundamental letters. I, 1.

אֵילָךְ *adv.* מִכַּאן וְאֵילָךְ hinc et ulterius; from now further. IV 16

אִלּוּ. These. Equals the biblical אֵלֶּה. VI. 1.

אֲלַכְסוֹן *adj.* [Greek λόξον] Oblique, diagonal direction. V, 2.

אֶמְעַע *n.* Middle. centre. I, 2.

ב

בּוּרִי *n.* Clearness, perspicuity. I, 3. וְהֶעֱמֵד דָּבָר עַל בּוּרִיוֹ and put the subject in a clear point of view.

בָּבָא *n.* Division. V, 6.

בֵּינוֹתָם or בְּנֹתַיִם Composed of בֵּין שְׁתוֹם, omitting ש between them. I, 1.
    [See Duke's Sprache der Mischnah, p. 68.]

ספר יצירה

ג

גַב *n.* Back. עַג גַּבֵּי upon the back id est, upon or above. VI, 8.

גוּף *n.* Body, substance II, 6.

גַלְגַל *n.* Circle, celestial orb, or sphere. II, 4.

ד

דִּבּוּר *n.* Word. I, 8.

ה

הִרְהֵר *v.* Think, muse. meditate, reflect. I, 7.

הִרְהוּר *n.* Reflection, meditation. V, 1.

ז

זְכוּת *n.* Innocence, purity, godliness, merit. II, 1.

ח

חוֹכָה *n.* Misdeed, trespass. II, 1.

חָזַר *v.* To return, to turn one's self round. II, 5.

חֲלִילָה *n.* Rotation; from חָל ל to dance round. II, 5.

ט

טָחוֹל *n.* Milt, spleen. V, 4.

כ

כָּאן *or* בַּאן *adv.* Here, there; מִכַּאן thence, from thence. IV, 16.

כּוֹכָב *n.* Star; especially the planet Mercury. IV, 7.

כִּיֵן *piel* כֵּיֵן *v.* Direct; מְכֻיָן directed, situated. I, 2.

כִּיעוּר *n.* Ugliness. IV, 3.

כָּךְ *or* לְכָךְ *adv.* So, thus. I, 7.

כָּרַע *Hiph.* הִכְרִיעַ *v.* To intervene in any thing, to mediate the peace, accomodate a quarrel. II, 1.

ל

לְעִימָה *n.* Eating, swallowing. V, 1.

לְפִיכָךְ *adv.* Composed of the words לְפִי and כָּךְ. According to that, therefore. IV, 15.

ספר יצירה

מ

מַאֲדִים *n.* The planet Mars. IV, 7.

מִדָּה *n.* Measure, quality, divine attribute. I, 4.

מִשְׁנָה *n.* Doctrine, lesson, paragraph.

מַזָלוֹת *n.* Constellations; especially the twelve signs of the Zodiac. V, 3. בְּמַזָּל מוֹ a happy constellation.

כְּמִין *adv.* It is a particle like כ, as; it is added the word מִין kind, denoting: as a kind of, like, as. II, 4.

מֵימַר *v.* Chald. inf. מֵמַר or מַאֲמָר. To speak, command. II, 5.

מַמָשׁ *n.* Substance, reality. II, 5.

מַעֲוִיבָה *n.* Rampart, a floor, pavement. I, 8.

מָרָה *n.* Gall. V, 4

מִתְנַהֵן See נָהַן. IV, 1.

נ

נָהַן *v.* With a ב following after it, signifies: to make use of any thing. IV, 1.

נוֹגַה *n.* The planet Venus. IV, 7.

נָעַץ *v.* Chald. Stick in, fasten, conjoin, connect. I, 6.

נָקַב *n.* Opening. IV, 8.

ס

סָדַר *v.* Arrange. V, 16.

סִימָן *n.* σημεῖον Sign, illustration. II, 4.

[See Geiger's Lesestücke der Mishnah, p. 121.]

סְלִיק *n.* Finished; the end (of a book or chapter.)

ע

יְבָהֵעֵר *n.* Contention, rivalry. V, 5.

עָתִיד *n.* Future. II, 2.

פ

פֶּרֶק *n.* Chapter, section.

פָּשׁוּם *adj.* Divested of clothes, undressed, simple. I, 8.

צ

צֶדֶק *n.* The planet Jupiter. IV, 7.

צְפִיָּה *n.* Appearance. I, 5.

צָרַף *v.* Refine, melt together, connect, combine. II, 2.

ספר יצירה

ק

קָבַע *v.* To fix, to fasten. I, 8. II, 3.
קֵבָה or קֵיבָה *n.* Stomach. V, 4.
קוּרְקְבָן or קַרְקְבָן *n.* Stomach. V, 4.

ר

רְאָיָה *n.* Argument, evidence. VI, 2.
רְאִיָה *n.* Sight. V, 1.
רְוָיָה *n.* Redundancy of water, moistness. III. 4.
רֵיחַ *v.* Smell. V, 1.

ש

שַׁבְתַאי *n.* The planet Saturn. IV, 7.
שִׂיחָה *n.* Speaking. V, 1.
שְׁמִיעָה *n.* Hearing. V, 1.
שֵׁרֵת *v.* To serve. I, 8.

ת

תְּלִי *n.* The constellation Draco or Dragon. VI, 2.

תַשְׁמִיש *n.* Coition. V, 1.

תָּפַם *or* תָּפַשׂ *v.* To seize, to take hold of.

ספר יצירה

Sepher Yetzirah   *Book of Creation*

The Aleph Bet

The Aleph Bet, the Hebrew Alphabet, has 22 letters (five of which appear in a different form at the end of a word) which are all consonants. Hebrew is written from right to left. During the years a system of vowels called nikud was added, but these are mostly seen in school books and prayer books. Newspapers, signs, magazines and most other printed materials in Israel today do not use nikud.

Letters of the Alefbet

א ב ג ד ה ו ז ח ט

Alef (Silent), Bet (B/V), Gimel (G), Dalet (D), He (H), Vav (V/O/U), Zayin (Z), Chet (Ch), Tet (T)

י כ ך ל מ ם נ ן ס

Yod (Y), Kaf (K/Kh), Khaf (Kh), Lamed (L), Mem (M), Mem (M), Nun (N), Nun (N), Samech (S)

ע פ ף צ ץ ק ר ש ת

Ayin (Silent), Pe (P/F), Fe (F), Tzade (Tz), Tzade (Tz), Qof (Q), Resh (R), Shin (Sh/S), Tav (T/S)

1	2	3	4	5	6	7	8	9
א	ב	ג	ד	ה	ו	ז	ח	ט
10	20	30	40	50	60	70	80	90
י	דכך	ל	מם	נן	ס	ע	פףפ	צץ
100	200	300	400					
ק	ר	שׁשׂ	ת					

Page 95

ספר יצירה

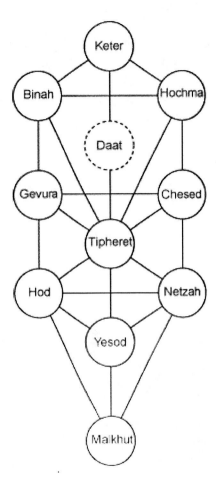

Tree of Life

Sepher Yetzirah   *Book of Creation*

SEFER YETZIRAH
Saaida Translation

Book of Creation

Translated by Saadia ben Joseph (892 CE)

ספר יצירה

Sepher Yetzirah *Book of Creation*

SEFER YETZIRAH

I. CHAPTER ONE.

1. In thirty-two mysterious paths of Wisdom, **Yah**, Eternal of Hosts [**Yod-Vav-Yod**], God of Israel, Living **Elohim**, Almighty God, High and Extolled, Dwelling in Eternity, Holy Be His Name, engraved and created His world in three **Sefarim**: in **writing**, **number** and **word**. Ten **Sefirot** out of nothing, twenty-two foundation letters, three mothers, seven doubles and twelve simples.

2. Ten **Sefirot** out of nothing according to the number of the ten digits [fingers and toes], which are five against five and a single covenant to be determined in the center. In word and tongue and mouth, they are ten extending beyond limit: depth of beginning, depth of end, depth of good, depth of evil, depth above and depth below, depth of east and depth of west, depth of north and depth of south, and the sole Master and lofty King faithfully governs them all from his Holy dwelling in Eternity forever.

3. Twenty-two foundation letters: three mothers, seven doubles and twelve simples. Three mothers: **Alef, Mem, Shin**: their basis is a scale of innocence and a scale of guilt and a tongue ordained to balance between the two. Seven doubles: **Bet, Gimel, Dalet, Kaf, Peh, Resh, Tav**. Their foundation is life and peace, wisdom and wealth, fruitfulness, grace and government. Twelve simples: **He, Vav, Zayin; Chet, Tet, Yod; Lamed, Nun, Samech; Ayin, Tsadeh, Qof**. Their foundation is seeing, hearing, smelling,

ספר יצירה

swallowing, copulating, acting, walking, raging, laughing, thinking, and sleeping.

4. By means of these media, **Yah**, Eternal of Hosts, God of Israel, Living **Elohim**, Almighty God, High and Extolled, Dwelling in Eternity, Holy Be His Name traced out [carved] three fathers and their posterity, seven conquerors and their hosts, and twelve diagonal boundaries. The proof of this is revealed in the universe, the year, and the soul, which rule ten, three, seven and twelve. Over them rule Tali (the dragon), the wheel, and the heart.

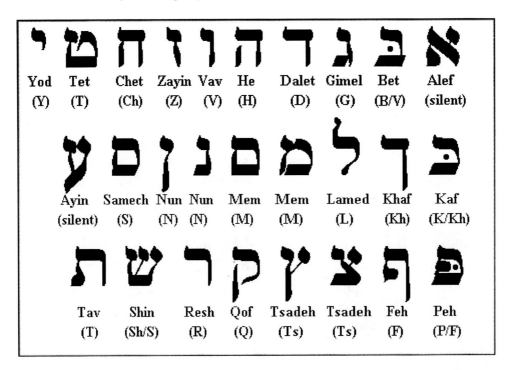

II. Chapter Two.

1. Ten **Sefirot** out of nothing. Ten and not nine, ten and not eleven. Understand in Wisdom and be wise in Understanding. Examine them, investigate them, think clearly and form. Place the word above its creator and reinstate a Creator upon His foundation; and they are ten extending beyond limit. Observe them: they appear like a flash. Their boundary has no limit for His word is with them: "and they ran and returned." And they pursue His saying like a whirlwind [vortex]; and they prostrate themselves [bend] themselves before His throne.

2. Twenty-two foundation letters: three mothers, seven doubles, and twelve simples. Three mothers: **Alef, Mem, Shin**: a great mystery, concealed, marvelous and magnificent whence emerge fire, wind [air, spirit, breath] and water, whence everything was created. Seven doubles: **Bet, Gimel, Dalet, Kaf, Peh, Resh, Tav**, which are to be pronounced in two tongues: **Bet, Vayt, Gimel, Ghimel, Dalet, Dhalet, Kaf, Khaf, Peh, Feh, Resh, Rhesh, Tav, Thav**, a pattern of hard and soft, strong and weak. The doubles represent the contraries [syzygies]. The opposite of life is death, the opposite of peace is evil [or 'harm'], the opposite of wisdom is foolishness, the opposite of wealth is poverty, the opposite of fruitfulness is barrenness, the opposite of grace is ugliness, the opposite of dominion is slavery.

3. Seven doubles: **Bet, Gimel, Dalet, Kaf, Peh, Resh, Tav**. Seven and not six, seven and not eight. Six sides in the six directions, and the Holy Palace [**Heikhal**] ruling in the center. Blessed is the

ספר יצירה

Eternal [**Yod-Vav-Yod**] in His dwelling. He is the place of the universe and the universe is not His place.

4. Twelve simples: **He, Vav, Zayin**; **Het, Tet, Yod**; **Lamed, Nun, Samech**; **Ayin, Tsadeh, Qof**. Twelve and not eleven, twelve and not thirteen. Twelve diagonal boundaries divide the directions and separate the different sides: the extremity of the northeast, the extremity of the eastern height, the extremity of the eastern depth, the extremity of the northwest, the extremity of the northern height, the extremity of the northern depth, the extremity of the southwest, the extremity of the western height, the extremity of the western depth, the extremity of the southeast, the extremity of the southern height, the extremity of the southern depth.

5. By these means, **Yah**, Eternal of Hosts, God of Israel, Living **Elohim**, Almighty God, High and Extolled, Dwelling in Eternity, Holy Be His Name traced twenty-two letters and fixed them upon a wheel. He turns the wheel forwards and backwards, and as a sign of this, nothing is better than to ascend in **delight** [**Ayin-Nun-Gimel**,], and nothing is worse than to descend with the **plague** [,**Nun-Gimel-Ayin**].

6. The proof of this is revealed in the universe, the year and the soul. The universe is calculated according to ten: the three are fire, air, and water; the seven are the seven planets; the twelve are the twelve signs of the zodiac. the year is computated by ten: the three are winter, summer and the seasons between; the seven are the seven days of creation; the twelve are the twelve months; the living soul is calculated according to ten: three are the head, chest and

stomach; seven are the seven apertures of the body; the twelve are the twelve leading organs.

ספר יצירה

Sepher Yetzirah *Book of Creation*

III. Chapter Three.

1. Ten **Sefirot** out of nothing. Stop your mouth from speaking, stop your heart from thinking, and if your heart runs (to think) return to a place of which it is said "they ran and returned"; and concerning this thing the covenant was made; and they are ten in extent beyond limit. Their end is infused with their beginning, and their beginning with their end like a flame attached to a glowing ember. Know, think [reflect, meditate] and imagine that the Creator is One and there is nothing apart from Him, and before One what do you count?

2. Twenty-two foundation letters: three mothers, seven doubles, and twelve simples. Three mothers: **Alef, Mem, Shin** are fire, wind [air] and water. The nature of the heavens is fire, the nature of air is wind [**ruach**], the nature of earth is water. Fire ascends and water descends and wind balances between the two. **Mem** is silent, **Shin** is sibilant, and **Alef** balances between the two. **Alef, Mem, Shin** are signed in six rings and enveloped in male and female. Know, meditate and imagine that the fire supports water.

3. Seven doubles: **Bet, Gimel, Dalet, Kaf, Peh, Resh, Tav** which are to be pronounced in two tongues: **Bet, Vet, Gimel, Ghimel, Dalet, Dhalet, Kaf, Khaf, Peh, Feh, Resh, Rhesh, Tav, Thav**, a pattern of hard and soft, strong and weak. The doubles represent the contraries. The opposite of life is death, the opposite of peace is evil, the opposite of wisdom is foolishness, the opposite of wealth is poverty, the opposite of fruitfulness is barrenness, the opposite of grace is ugliness, the opposite of dominion is slavery.

ספר יצירה

4. Twelve simples: **He, Vav, Zayin**; **Het, Tet, Yod**; **Lamed, Nun, Samech**; **Ayin, Tsadeh, Qof**. He engraved them, hewed them, tested them, weighed them, and exchanged them. How did He combine them? Two stones build two houses. Three stones build six houses. Four stones build twenty-four houses. Five stones build one hundred twenty houses. Six stones build seven hundred twenty houses. Seven stones build five thousand forty houses. Thenceforth, go out and calculate what the mouth is unable to say and what the ear is unable to hear.

5. Through these media, **Yah**, Eternal of Hosts, God of Israel, Living **Elohim**, Almighty Master, Lofty and Extolled, Dwelling in Eternity, Holy Be His Name traced [carved] (His universe). **Yah [Yod-He]** is composed of two letters; **YHVH [Yod-He-Vav-He]** is composed of four letters; Hosts **[Tsvaot]**: it is like a signal [sign, ot] in his army [tsava]; God of Israel: Israel is a prince [Sar] before God [El]; Living **Elohim**: three things are called living, Living **Elohim**, the water of life and the Tree of Life; **El [Alef-Lamed]**: strength, **Shaddai [Shin-Dalet-Yod]**: He is sufficient to this point; Lofty [**Ram**]: because He dwells in the heights of the universe and is above all elevated being; Extolled [**Nisah**]: because He carries and maintains the height and depth whilst the bearers are below and their burden is above. He carries and maintains the entire creation; Dwelling in Eternity [**Shochen ahd**]: because His reign is eternal and uninterrupted; Holy Be His Name[**Qadosh Shmo**]: because He and His servants are sacred and they declare unto Him every day: Holy, Holy, Holy.

6. The proof of this is revealed in the universe, the year and the soul. The twelve are below, the seven are above them, and the three are above the seven. Of the three, He has formed His sanctuary and all are attached to the One: a sign of the One who has no second, a solitary King in His Universe is One, and His Name is One.

ספר יצירה

Sepher Yetzirah   *Book of Creation*

IV. Chapter Four.

1. Ten **Sefirot** out of nothing. One: Spirit-wind of the Living **Elohim,** Life of the Universe, whose throne strengthens all eternity, Blessed and Beneficent Be His Name, constant and eternal: this is the Holy Spirit.

2. Spirit from Spirit engraved and hewed: He cut the four dimensions of Heaven: the east, the west, the north and the south, and there is a wind for each direction.

3. Twenty-two foundation letters: three mothers, seven doubles, and twelve simples. He hewed them in spirit, carved them in voice, fixed them in the mouth in five place: **Alef, He, Het, Ayin** [ahacha]; **Bet, Vav, Mem, Feh** [bumaf]; **Gimel, Yod, Khaf, Qof** [gikhaq]; **Dalet, Tet, Lamed, Nun, Tav** [datlanat]; **Zayin, Samech, Tsadeh, Resh, Shin** [zsats'ras]. **Alef, He, Het, Ayin** are pronounced at the end of the tongue at the place of swallowing; **Bet, Vav, Mem, Feh** between the teeth with the tip of the tongue; **Gimel, Yod, Khaf, Qof** on the palate; **Dalet, Tet, Lamed, Nun, Tav** on the middle of the tongue and pronounced with the voice; **Zayin, Samech, Tsadeh, Resh, Shin** between the teeth with the tongue at rest.

4. Twenty-two letters: He carved them, hewed them, refined them, weighed them, and combined them, and He made of them the entire creation and everything to be created in the future. How did He test them? **Alef** with all and all with **Alef, Bet** with all and all with **Bet, Gimel** with all and all with **Gimel,** and they all return again and

ספר יצירה

again, and they emanate through two hundred and thirty-one gates. All the words and all the creatures emanate from One Name.

5. He created reality from **Tohu [Tav-He-Vav]** and made His existence out of His nothingness, and He hewed great pillars from the intangible air.

6. Three: water of spirit carved and hewed of it **Tohu [Tav-He-Vav]** and **Bohu [Bet-He-Vav]**, mud and clay. He made them like a garden bed, put them into position like a wall and covered them like a fortification. he poured water upon them and made dust, for He saith to the snow: be earth. (**Tohu**: this is the green line which encircles the entire world; **Bohu**: this refers to the rocks split and submerged in the abyss where the water has its source.) As it is said: He spread out the line of **Tohu** and the rocks of **Bohu** upon it [the water].

7. Four: fire from water, He engraved and hewed from it a throne of glory and the host dwelling in the heights, as it is written: Who maketh the winds His messengers, the flames of fire His ministers.

8. Five: He chose three simples and fixed them to His great Name, and with them He sealed six extremities. He sealed the height, turning upwards and sealed it with **Yod-He-Vav**. Six: He sealed the depth and He turned below and sealed it with **Yod-Vav-He**. Seven: he sealed the east and turned forwards, and sealed it with **He-Vav-Yod**. Eight: He sealed the west and turned backwards and sealed it with **He-Yod-Vav**. Nine: He sealed the south and turned to His right and sealed it with **Vav-Yod-He**. Ten: He sealed the north and

turned to His left and sealed it with **Vav-He-Yod**. These are the ten **Sefirot** out of nothing, One: Spirit of the Living **Elohim**; two: wind of the spirit; three: water of the wind; four: fire from the water, height and depth, east and west, north and south.

ספר יצירה

V. Chapter Five.

1. He made the letter **Alef** King in Spirit and bound to it a crown and tested this one with this one, and formed of it: air in the universe, abundant moisture in the year, and body in the soul, male and female; with the male: **Alef, Mem, Shin**, and with the female: **Alef, Shin, Mem**.

2. He made the letter **Mem** King in Spirit and bound to it a crown and tested this one with this one, and formed of it: earth in the universe, cold in the year, and belly in the soul (male and female).

3. He made the letter **Shin** King in Spirit and bound to it a crown and tested this one with this one, and formed of it: Heaven in the universe, heat in the year, and head in the soul, male and female. How did He combine them? **Alef, Mem, Shin, Alef, Shin, Mem, Mem, Shin, Alef, Mem, Alef, Shin, Shin, Alef, Mem, Shin, Mem, Alef.** Heaven is from fire, the atmosphere is from air, the earth is from water. The head of Adam is fire, his heart is of the spirit-wind, and his stomach is from water.

4. Seven doubles: **Bet, Gimel, Dalet, Kaf, Peh, Resh, Tav.** He carved them, hewed them, tested them, weighed them, and combined them. He made of them: the planets, the days (of the week), and the apertures (of the head).

5. He made the letter **Bet** King and bound to it a crown and tested this one with this one, and formed of it: Saturn in the universe, the Sabbath in the year, and the mouth in the soul.

ספר יצירה

6. He made the letter **Gimel** King and bound to it a crown and tested this one with this one, and formed of it: Jupiter in the universe, Sunday in the year, and the right eye of the soul.

7. He made the letter **Dalet** King and bound to it a crown and tested this one with this one, and formed of it: Mars in the universe, Monday in the year, and the left eye of the soul.

8. He made the letter **Kaf** King and bound to it a crown and tested this one with this one, and formed of it: Sun in the universe, Tuesday in the year, and the right nostril of the soul.

9. He made the letter **Peh** King and bound to it a crown and tested this one with this one, and formed of it: Venus in the universe, Wednesday in the year, and the left nostril of the soul.

10. He made the letter **Resh** King and bound to it a crown and tested this one with this one, and formed of it: Mercury in the universe, Thursday in the year, and the right ear of the soul.

11. He made the letter **Tav** King and bound to it a crown and tested this one with this one, and formed of it: Moon in the universe, Friday in the year, and the left ear of the soul.

12. He separated the witnesses and He bestowed a portion to each of them: a portion to the universe, a portion to the year, and a portion to the soul.

VI. Chapter Six.

Twelve simples: **He, Vav, Zayin**; **Het, Tet, Yod**; **Lamed, Nun, Samech**; **Ayin, Tsadeh, Qof**. He carved them, hewed them, tested them, weighed them, and combined them. He formed of them: the signs of the zodiac, the months [of the year], and the leading organs of the body; two are agitated, two are tranquil, two are advising, and two are joyous (these are the two intestines), the two hands, and the two feet.

1. He made them like contenders and set them up like a kind of war; **Elohim** made them one against the other.

2. Three, to each a portion; seven divided into three above, three [below], and the one rules as a balance between the two. Twelve are arranged in battle: three are friends, three are enemies, three are murderers, and three are resurrectors; and they all are attached one to another. As a sign of this thing, twenty-two inclinations and one body.

3. How did He combine them? **He, Vav, Vav, He; Zayin, Het, Het, Zayin; Tet, Yod, Yod, Tet; Lamed, Nun, Nun, Lamed; Samech, Ayin , Ayin, Samech; Tsadeh, Qof, Qof, Tsadeh**.

4. He made the letter **He** King and bound to it a crown and tested this one with this one, and formed of it: Aries in the universe, Nisan in the year, and the liver of the soul.

ספר יצירה

5. He made the letter **Vav** King and bound to it a crown and tested this one with this one, and formed of it: Taurus in the universe, Iyyar in the year, and the gall-bladder of the soul.

6. He made the letter **Zayin** King and bound to it a crown and tested this one with this one, and formed of it: Gemini in the universe, Sivan in the year, and the spleen in the soul.

7. He made the letter **Het** King and bound to it a crown and tested this one with this one, and formed of it: Cancer in the universe, Tammuz in the year, and the intestine in the soul.

8. He made the letter **Tet** King and bound to it a crown and tested this one with this one, and formed of it: Leo in the universe, Ab in the year, and the right kidney in the soul.

9. He made the letter **Yod** King and bound to it a crown and tested this one with this one, and formed of it: Virgo in the universe, Elul in the year, and the left kidney in the soul.

10. He made the letter **Lamed** King and bound to it a crown and tested this one with this one, and formed of it: Libra in the universe, Tishri in the year, and the intestines in the soul.

11. He made the letter **Nun** King and bound to it a crown and tested this one with this one, and formed of it: Scorpio in the universe, Marheshvan in the year, and the stomach in the soul.

12. He made the letter **Samech** King and bound to it a crown and tested this one with this one, and formed of it: Sagittarius in the universe, Kislev in the year, and the right hand of the soul.

13. He made the letter **Ayin** King and bound to it a crown and tested this one with this one, and formed of it: Capricorn in the universe, Tevet in the year, and the left hand of the soul.

14. He made the letter **Tsadeh** King and bound to it a crown and tested this one with this one, and formed of it: Aquarius in the universe, Shvat in the year, and the right foot of the soul.

15. He made the letter **Qof** King and bound to it a crown and tested this one with this one, and formed of it: Pisces in the universe, Adar in the year, and the left foot of the soul.

16. He divided the witnesses and bestowed a portion to each of them: a portion to the universe, a portion to the year, and a portion to the soul.

ספר יצירה

VII. Chapter Seven.

1. Air, between seasons ["abundant moisture"], trunk [i.e. torso]. --- Earth, cold, belly. --- Heaven, heat [summer], the head: these are **Alef**, **Mem** and **Shin**.

2. Saturn, Sabbath, the mouth. --- Jupiter, Sunday, right eye. --- Mars, Monday, left eye. --- The Sun, Tuesday, right nostril. --- Venus, Wednesday, left nostril. --- Mercury, Thursday, right ear. --- Moon, Friday, left ear: these are **Bet**, **Gimel**, **Dalet**, **Kaf**, **Peh**, **Resh** and **Tav**.

3. Aries, Nisan, liver. ---Taurus, Iyyar, gall-bladder. ---Gemini, Sivan, spleen. --- Cancer, Tammuz, intestine. --- Leo, Ab, right kidney. --- Virgo, Elul, left kidney. --- Libra, Tishri, intestines. --- Scorpio, Marheshvan, stomach. --- Sagittarius, Kislev, right hand. --- Capricorn, Tevet, left hand. --- Aquarius, Shvat, right foot. --- Pisces, Adar, left foot: and these are **He**, **Vav**, **Zayin**; **Het**, **Tet**, **Yod**; **Lamed**, **Nun**, **Samech**; **Ayin**, **Tsadeh**, **Qof**.

ספר יצירה

VIII. Chapter Eight.

With **Alef** have been formed: the spirit-wind, air, the between seasons, the chest, the tongue. With **Mem** have been formed: water, earth, cold, belly, and the balance of guilt. With **Shin** have been formed: fire, Heaven, heat, the head, and the balance of innocence. With **Bet** have been formed: Saturn, the Sabbath, life and death. With **Gimel** have been formed: Jupiter, Sunday, the right eye, peace and harm. With **Dalet** have been formed: Mars, Monday, the left eye, wisdom and foolishness. With **Kaf** have been formed: the Sun, Tuesday, the right nostril, wealth and poverty. With **Peh** have been formed: Venus, Wednesday, the left nostril, fertility and desolation [barrenness]. With **Resh** have been formed: Mercury, Thursday, the right ear, grace and ugliness. With **Tav** have been formed: the Moon, Friday, the left ear, dominion and slavery. With **He** have been formed: Aries, Nisan, the liver, vision and blindness. With **Vav** have been formed: Taurus, Iyyar, the spleen, hearing and deafness. With **Zayin** have been formed: Gemini, Sivan, the gall, odor and odorlessness. With **Het** have been formed: Cancer, Tammuz, the intestine, the word and silence. With **Tet** have been formed: Leo, Ab, the right kidney, eating and hunger. With **Yod** have been formed: Virgo, Elul, the left kidney, copulating and castration. With **Lamed** have been formed: Libra, Tishri, the intestines, acting and impotence. With **Nun** have been formed: Scorpio, Marheshvan, the gullet, walking and limping. With **Samech** have been formed: Sagittarius, Kislev, the right hand, rage and loss of faith. With **Ayin** have been formed: Capricorn, Tevet, the left hand, laughing and the loss of spleen. With **Tsadeh** have

ספר יצירה

been formed: Aquarius, Shvat, the right foot, thinking and loss of heart. With **Qof** have been formed: Pisces, Adar, the left foot, sleeping and languor. And they are all fixed to the Dragon [Tali], the wheel, and the heart. Tali in the universe is like a king upon his throne, the wheel in the year is like a king in his empire, and the heart in the body is like a king at war. To recapitulate: some reunited with the others, and those reunited with the former. These are opposed to those and those are opposed to these. These are the contrary of those and those are the contrary of these. If these are not, those are not. And if those are not, these are not; and they are all fixed to Tali [the Dragon], the wheel and the heart.

And when Abraham our father had formed and combined and investigated and reckoned and succeeded, then **He-Qof-Bet-He**, "The Holy One Blessed Be He" was revealed unto him, and unto Abraham He called this convocation: "Before I formed thee in the belly, I knew thee, and before thou left the womb, I sanctified thee, and I placed thee like a prophet amidst the nations." And He made Abraham a beloved friend, and cut a covenant with him and his seed forever and ever.

Commentary on Sefer Yetzirah

by Saadia ben Joseph (al-Fayyumi) [931 C.E.]

Saadia's Commentary

[From Saadia ben Joseph (al-Fayyumi), **Commentaire sur le Séfer Yesira ou Livre de la Création par Le Gaon Saadya de Fayyoum**, trans. & ed., M. Lambert, Paris, Emile Bouillon, Editeur, 1891);

ספר יצירה

Sepher Yetzirah   *Book of Creation*

I. On the Origin of the World According to the Pythagoreans & the Sefer Yetzirah

... The seventh system belongs to the theorist who admits a creation of things, but asserts that the first things created were numbers. By means of numbers, substances and particles are differentiated. Geometry and figures are based on number, for all created things necessarily have some kind of form. According to this theory, the figure of the created object precedes the object itself, for it is the object's material. However, if this theorist---may God have mercy upon you!---supposes the potential, and not actual, anteriority of numbers to numbered things, then we must accept this as a just and irrefutable theory. We maintain that the number, in potentiality, has prefigured the numbered object; that the form has preceded the formed thing; the figure, the figured thing; geometry, the geometrical body; and composition, the thing composed---all in potentiality and not in actuality. But if this theory posits the actual anteriority of pure numbers, isolated compositions, and abstract theorems, the supposition is inadmissible for two reasons: (1) the theory implies that the Mover and the moved were joined by a third thing: motion; with the forming agent and the formed object, it names another object: form; and along with the Creator and his creature, it posits a necessary third: creation. This is absurd; (2) it is contradictory to speak of abstract composition and pure theorem, for these are necessarily based upon at least two terms.

The eighth system belongs to the theorist who accepts a creation, but ascribes the origin of things to numbers and letters. This theory belongs to the author of this book. In fact, he ascribes the origin of

ספר יצירה

the Creator's creation to thirty-two things: the ten numbers and twenty-two letters. He does not say, however, that they are abstract and isolated. He only says that God has created the air and has established the thirty-two things in it. The numbers, according to him, traverse the air, which is composed of distinct particles. When the air current follows these direct and inflected lines, it produces figures. After examining this theory, we find these points to be correct, but they need to be completed by the following exposition. The same applies to the letters. When their creator established them in the air, they were cleaved, and figures of diverse appearance and geometrical forms were created according to the faculty of each isolated letter, two letters combined, or one compound of numerous letters.

Our rabbis say something similar with regard to the scene at Mt. Sinai in the Scripture, for it is said: "And all the people saw the thunderings," [Exodus XX, 15]. The rabbis asked how it was possible to see sounds? They explained that the Sage brought a powerful and brilliant fire down upon the mountain, as it is said: "Because the Eternal descended upon it in fire," [Exodus XIX, 18]. Then He surrounded it with a black cloud, "and the mountain burned with fire unto the midst of heaven, with darkness, clouds, and thick darkness," [Deuteronomy IV, 11]. This darkness is the black cloud, as it is said: "He made darkness his secret place; his pavillion round about him were dark waters and thick clouds of the skies," [Psalms XLVIII, 12]. Thus did He create the scintillating voice in the fire; the voice emanated from fire and its form appeared in the cloud according to the impulsion given by the pronunciation's movement in the air. The people saw this form and knew then that the fire's scintillation had projected it into the surrounding black air, as it is said: "And the Eternal spoke unto you out of the midst of the fire,"[Deuteronomy IV, 12], and it is said: "when ye heard the voice out of the midst of the darkness," [Deuteronomy V, 23]. As an example of this, we see that when someone speaks on a cold day, the articulation of the voice cuts the air and produces forms varying in straight or inflected lines according to the current which the sounds follow. Similarly, the author says that numbers and letters are the origins of things; he means with the air, as we have just demonstrated. [. . .]

ספר יצירה

Sepher Yetzirah   *Book of Creation*

II. On the Divine Epithets and the Aristotelian Categories

What do the ten names of God enumerated at the beginning signify and why does the author limit himself to one? The names of God, like the names of all beings, refer to actual or alleged events. In the **Ma'aseh bereshit** [Work of Creation], God is called **Elohim**, the name of essence. He is not called Eternal [Adonai, **Yod-Vav-Yod**] before the creation of the creatures, because to be Lord, He must be the Master of someone. The Sages have said: "He has mentioned a full name for a full world," [**Beresit Rabba**, XIII]. He is called **El Shaddai** ["Almighty God," Genesis, XVII, 1] when He orders Abraham's circumcision and says: count on me who helps and saves.

He called Himself "I am that I am," [**Ehyeh asher ehyeh**, Exodus III, 14] when He produced the miracles and marvels like the phenomena of creation, the ten plagues and the rest. He is the One who realizes but cannot be realized. He called Himself **Yah** [**Yod-He**] when He produced the extraordinary miracles on the Red Sea. He called Himself **Elohim Hayyim** ["Living God"] when He revealed His voice to the people and they heard, and did not die but were given life, as it is said: "For who is there of all flesh that hath heard the voice of the living God," [Deuteronomy, V, 26]. He called Himself **Adonai Sabaoth** ["Eternal (or Lord) of Hosts"] when the people's pilgrimage and assembly in the sanctuary was recounted, as it is said: "And this man went up out of his city yearly to worship and to sacrifice unto the Eternal of hosts in Shiloh," [I Samuel I, 3]. He is called High and Extolled [**Ram v'Nisah**] when Isaiah speaks of Uzziah, king of Judah: "In the year that king

ספר יצירה

Uzziah died I saw the Lord sitting upon a throne, high and lifted up," [Isaiah VI, 1]. On account of Uzziyahu, he has said: "But when he was strong his heart was lifted up to his destruction: for he transgressed against the Lord his God," [II Chronicles XXVI, 16]. He called Himself Lord **[Adon]** when He announced that He would raise the noble among the people, for it is said: "For behold the Lord, the Lord of Hosts doth take way from Jerusalem," Isaiah III, 1]. He is most often called Eternal God **[Yod-Vav-Yod Elohim]** in the books of Jeremiah and Ezekiel, and not Eternal of Hosts **[Yod-Vav-Yod Tsvaot (Sabaoth)]** because Israel's legions had been dispersed and His totality had been fragmented. When the Israelites gathered in the second temple, He called Himself Eternal of Hosts, and this appellation is always used in the prophecies of Haggai, Zechariah, and Malachi. Only once is He called Eternal God of Israel. This is in the verse: "Let him send her away saith the Eternal, the God of Israel," [Malachi II, 16]. This name can be understood in a general and a restricted sense. In the restricted sense, the law of divorce can be applied to the Israelite only by another Israelite, and not by the pagans. If the pagans compel the divorce, it is nullified. In the general sense of the word, it refers to the Lord's possession of Israel. Though Israel has been chased and exiled, the Lord has neither abandoned nor forsaken her, but considers her His own. He has been called "changeth the times and the seasons," [Daniel II, 21] when He transforms the era of domination into one of servitude. He has been called "He removeth kings and setteth up kings," [Daniel II, 21] when He dethroned Sedecias and made Nebuchadnezzar king. He has been called: "He giveth wisdom unto the wise," [Daniel II, 21] because He taught wisdom to Daniel. He has been called "He revealeth the deep and secret things" [Daniel II, 22] for He revealed the nature of vision to Daniel. Finally, it is said: "And Esdras blessed the Lord, the Great God," [Nehemiah VIII, 6], for God has said: "The glory of this latter house shall be greater than of the former," [Haggai II, 9].

The names of angels correspond in like manner to events which are the angel's task to realize. When God dispatched angels to Abraham to announce the glad tidings, they resembled and were thus called "men" [**anashim**, Genesis XVIII, 2]. When God sent the angels to destroy Sodom, they were called "angels" [**malachim**, Genesis XIX, 1]. When God sent them unto Isaiah to burn him with hot coal because he neglected to warn Israel, they were called "**seraphim**" as it is said: "Then flew one of the seraphim unto me having a live coal in his hand....and he laid it upon my mouth," [Isaiah VI, 6-7]. When Ezekiel saw them in the form of unreasoning animals, they were called "**hayyot**" ["creatures," Ezekiel I, 5]. The angels between them, which turned not when they went, were called "**ophanim**," ["wheels," Ezekiel I, 15]. The most elevated between them have been called "cherubim" [Ezekiel X, 1] because each elevated being among men is called "cherub," as it is said of the king of Tyre: "Thou wast the annointed Cherub that covereth," [Ezekiel XXVIII, 14].

The names of the celestial bodies vary according to their different characteristics. The one with a bright light in the center is called "bright" [or "luminary"] as it is said: "All the bright lights," [Ezekiel XXXII, 8], according to the term for the Sun. The star with lesser brilliance is called "**Nogah**" ["shining"] after a name for the Moon, as it has been said: "neither for brightness shall the moon

ספר יצירה

give light unto thee," [Isaiah LX, 19]. **Nogah** is also the Hebrew name for Venus. Stars with a hot nature are called **"Kesilim"** ["constellations" and "Orion"], as it is said: "For the stars of heaven and the constellations" [Isaiah XIII, 10]. This refers to the name Orion, which is **Kesil** and its fires. Luminaries with a cold nature are called **Mazzaroth** ["Pleiades"], as it is said: "Canst thou bring forth Mazzaroth in his seasons?" [Job XXXVIII, 32]. Israel's different names of praise such as Jacob, Israel, and Jeshurun [Deuteronomy XXXII, 15]; and her different names of blame like **"M'shuva"** ["backsliding," Jeremiah III, 6], **"B' gedah"** ["treacherous," Jeremiah III, 8], **"Oholah"** and **"Oholibah"** [Ezekiel XXIII, 4] correspond to particular events. These names of the angels, luminaries, and the nation are an interpretation of actual characteristics. The names of the Creator, however, are only indications and extractions [abstractions] of his powers ---may He be praised and exalted!

The author of our book intends to show us how the existence of beings is realized. When the wise grasped this knowledge, they discovered the ten and only ten categories which reason can use to order all things: substance, quantity, quality, relation, space, time, possession, position, action, and passivity. When the sages precisely established these ten categories, no conception remained unconnected to them except the idea of the Creator, for He is above all intuition and comprehension. Therefore, our author has enumerated these ten categories at the beginning of his book in a style befitting the rest of his exposition. The name **Yah** refers to substance [essence] for the author translates it as Eternal, and he derives it from the word **hayyot** [being or creature] and **'hayu"** ["they have been"]. This name applies to eternity, and God is the Creator of all substances. The name Eternal **Sabaoth** [Eternal of Hosts] corresponds to the categories of action and passivity. The Eternal is active, as it is said: "I am the Eternal that maketh all things," [Isaiah XLIV, 24]. The passive, which is great in number, is called "legion" [host or armies]. The name Living God [**Elohim Hayyim**] refers to Elohim as the Creator of quantity, for the measure of life (i.e., age) is a quantitative measure. The name **El Shaddai** ["Almighty God"] refers to God the Creator of quality, for the name **Shaddai** [Shin-Dalet-Yod] derives from "**dai**"[Dalet-Yod, "sufficient"] and "**daim**" [Dalet-Yod-Mem, "sufficiently"]. The name **Elohei Israel**, God of Israel, refers to relation. The name Lofty [**Ram**] refers to God as Creator of the Good, while the name **Nisah** ["elevated"] refers to the category of position. The name **Shokhen Ad** ["dwelling in eternity"] indicates the time before and after which He is; and finally, the epithet **Qadosh Shmo** ["Holy be His Name"] refers to the category of possession and to the noble attributes which allow our intelligence to reach an approximate idea of Him. Therefore, the ten names clearly suit the ten categories, and according to our author, there remains nothing which God has not created.

After a deep examination and detailed analysis, we conclude that the Ten Commandments heard by our fathers before Mt. Sinai correspond to these same ten categories which encompass every precept. The commandment "I am the Eternal" alludes to the category of action, as it is said: "I am the Eternal that maketh all things," [Isaiah XLIV, 24]. The commandment "Thou shalt have no

ספר יצירה

other gods..." refers to substance, for it adds: "that is in heaven above or that is in the earth beneath or that is in the water under the earth." The commandment "Thou shalt not take (the name of the Lord in vain) refers to quality since most oaths only apply to modes of being. The commandment: "Remember the Sabbath day" explicitly relates to the category of time. The commandment: "Honor thy father and thy mother" is the relation itself. The commandment: "Thou shalt not kill" indicates the category of passivity, as it is said: "for in the image of God made He man" [Genesis IX, 6]. The commandment: "Thou shalt not commit adultery" designates the category of position, for this act is a kind of position and contact. The commandment: "Thou shalt not steal" directly corresponds to possession. The commandment: "Thou shalt not bear false witness" refers to quantity since most false witnessing applies to measurement. Finally, the commandment: "Thou shalt not covet" indicates space and everything corresponding to it; thus the Sage adds: "the house of thy neighbor." Therefore, the decalogue clearly comprehends all the notions in the world. By the same token, the 613 precepts must therefore be contained in the decalogue without exception.

By co-ordinating these precepts in accordance with the Ten Commandments, I have discovered that 80 precepts correspond to the first commandment, 60 precepts correspond to the second commandment, 48 correspond to the third, 75 to the fourth, 77 to the fifth, 50 to the sixth, 58 to the seventh, 59 to the eighth, 52 to the ninth, and 54 to the tenth. This amounts to 613. There are 620 letters in the decalogue, of which 613 correspond to the 613 precepts. The remaining seven letters are contained in the two concluding words: "that is your neighbor's," but they are already subsumed in the words immediately before them: "nor anything" [Exodus XX, 17]. Blessed be the Sage who put so many things in so few words!

The words [from **Sefer Yetzirah**] "He created His world in three **sefarim**" indicate the three ways of recording all things. The sages counted four aspects: substance, word, writing or thought. For example, we see a man in substance; or we say the word: "man"; or we write the letters: M A N; or we represent an image of the man in thought. Now why does our author only enumerate three aspects of a thing? He calls them "three **sefarim**" ["three books"] or "three divans," and these are: scripture, number and word. When the category of substance is added to them, they comprise the four aspects. Substance and thought do not vary. Viewed according to these two categories, the object makes the same impression on all men. The other two aspects, scripture and word, do vary, for we see many different languages and scripts. However, the ideas underlying these are not different. [. . .]

ספר יצירה

III. On the "Closed" Numbers, Mothers, Doubles, & Simples:

The author then explains the thirty-two paths, and says that these are ten numbers and twenty-two letters. We translate the word "**b'limah**" as "closed." The proper sense is: 'provided with a brake,' as it is said: "whose mouth must be held in with bit and bridle," [Psalms XXXII, 9]. The author then divides the letters into "three fundamental mothers". The sense of the word [**Alef-Vav-Mem, ôm**] is "mother" and this is a term in the Mishna. It is said: "There is one mother for the tradition and one mother for the reading" [Pesahim 6b; Sukkah 6b]. This means that the Law has been interpreted in two ways: according to the principle of the Scripture and according to the principle of oral lecture. The word [ôm] is called the primitive origin of the body part where leprosy resides, as in the passage: "either the primitive origin of the wound has disappeared or dimished" [Nega'im, I, 5]. Using this metaphor, the author says "three fundamental letters" [**yesod gimel otiot**].

The proper sense of the words "**sheva k'phulot**" is "seven doubles," for it is said that there are two kinds of knowledge: "the secrets of wisdom, that they are double to that which is" [Job XI, 6]. This is the knowledge of the Creator and the knowledge of the creature. There are also two kinds of punishments: "for she [Jerusalem] hath received of the Lord's hand double for all her sins" [Isaiah XL, 2]. These are the punishments in person and fortune, of the sacred and the profane, for the king and the multitude, and among the distinguished and the vulgar.

ספר יצירה

The words "**shtem esre ph'shutot**" indicate the "twelve simple" letters. With respect to composed objects, isolated and separate things are called "simple" to distinguish them from compounds, as it is said: "a simple year" to distinguish it from the embolismic year. The simple year is of twelve months, the embolismic year has thirteen months. One also says "first born" and "simple". "First born" refers to two parts, and "simple" to one part. In astronomical charts of complex years, this is an approximate measure of a certain star's revolution. The simple years are the average of its progression through each solar year. Since the seven letters are double, the remaining letters are called simple to distinguish them from the compound... [. . .]

IV. On the Creation's "Witnesses"

"By means of these [32 paths], the Eternal, Master of armies, God of Israel, living Elohim, Almighty, Unique, Lofty and Dwelling in Eternity, Holy Be His Name has traced three mothers and their progeny, seven chiefs and their armies, and twelve limits of the angle. Proof of this is given by the trustworthy witnesses: the universe, the year and the person [soul]. To each applies the rule of ten, three, seven and twelve and their correspondents: the sphere, the Dragon and the heart. [Chapter One, 4].

I translate "fathers" [**avot**] as "mothers", for as I have previously stated, the words: fathers, mothers, principals, materia prima, initial substance, etc. all have the same meaning. I translate the word "**kobeshin**" as "chiefs" because they conquer countries, as it is said: "And shall consume the earth before the Eternal," [Deuteronomy XXXII, 22]. Elsewhere it is said: "of all the nations which he had subdued," [II Samuel VIII, 11]. I translate the words "**g'vulei alakson**" as "limit of the angles" because this is the sense of the words frequently found in the Talmud. There it is said: "every cubit forms a cubit and two-fifths in diagonal" [Baba Batra, 101 b]. This means that the diagonal is one and two-fifths cubits in every square with a simple side of one cubit, though this is not quite correct. The exact measure of the diagonal is the square root of two.

Tali [Tav-Lamed-Yod] can be defined as the dragon. I understand this to be the place where two orbits intersect [the orbit of the sun and the orbit of the moon] like the equator and the sun's orbit.

ספר יצירה

Actually, the circle of the sun's orbit is inclined twenty-three degrees and a fraction to the circle of the equator. When we suppose that the two orbits are aligned, they necessarily intersect at two opposite points. One of the two points is called the spring equinox and the other, the autumnal equinox. Just as the solar and lunar orbits intersect one another at two opposite points (each point called "dragon"), one of these points is sometimes called the head, and the other, the tail. This explains the origin of the dragon's name. It is not a constellation resembling a dragon or any other creature. "Dragon" refers to the coils and curves which it forms when one sphere is positioned in the north and the other in the south. The Hebrews have given it a similar name, since it is said: "By his spirit hath he garnished the heavens; His hand hath formed the crooked serpent...."

Sepher Yetzirah   Book of Creation

V. On the Geometrical "Whirlwind" of the Hebrew Letters

"The ten closed numbers are ten and not nine, nor eleven; understand in wisdom and ponder them in intelligence; know, reflect and believe; situate the thing according to its evidence and establish the Creator according to its quality. The numbers correspond to ten infinities, whose beginning flashes like lightning; but one finds no end to them when searching for their limit; and the decree of the Creator made them like angels who ran and returned; and they pursue his decree like a whirlwind, and it is as if they would prostrate themselves before his throne."[Chapter Two; 1.]

. . .Of the two statements which follow the three propositions, the first is: "His decree is with them, and they ran and returned." The author's meaning is that every time the numbers arrive at ten, they return and begin again eternally and without limit for us, as it is also said of the angels: "And the living creatures ran and returned as the appearance of a flash of lightning" [Ezekiel I, 14]. They return and then depart again, and it is as if they had been stationary, as it is said: "Canst thou send lightnings, that they may go, and say unto thee, here we are?" [Job XXXVIII, 35]. They have faces on all sides, and thus it is said: "And behold, the angel that talked with me went forth, and another angel went out to meet him," [Zechariah II, 3]. It is not said that the angel appeared "behind him" because the angel presents a face every direction it turns. Like the numbers, the letters also always repeat themselves, following and succeeding without an end for us.

ספר יצירה

The second of the two statements is: "And they pursue his speech like a whirlwind." The author's intention here is to emphasize how the letters and numbers are formed in the air. He says that the whirlwinds describe figures and forms in the air, and though they all differ, they are still all circular. Among their material forms, some are more oblong, others combine circle and square, others combine circle and triangle, some are composed of superimposed spheres, and still others are composed of interpenetrating spheres. All of these are types of whirlwind. This analogy explains how the letters and numbers are formed and have sprung into the air; and this is why it is said: "The Eternal hath his way in the whirlwind and in the storm," [Nahum I, 3]; and also: "For behold, the Eternal will come with fire, and with his chariots like a whirlwind" [Isaiah LXVI,15]. Ezekiel demonstrated this with respect to the **ophanim** and the **hayyot**; the circles [or 'wheels'--trans.] interpenetrate like tubes within tubes. The same thing can be said for the junction of whirlwind within whirlwind and tempest within tempest. Thus it is clear that God ---be He celebrated and exalted---has revealed the lights of the hayyot and the ophanim which have circular forms. The prophets were also shown winds which have the same circular forms, as it has been said: "Then the Eternal answered Job out of the whirlwind" [Job XXXVIII, 1], and elsewhere: "out of the whirlwind" [Job XL, 6]. If one has properly comprehended the formation of the letters in the air, this will not seem difficult. As for the saying: "They prostrate themselves before His throne," [it only alludes to the numbers and letters obeying him and executing his decrees. The word "prostrate" should not be understood in the literal sense....

Sepher Yetzirah   *Book of Creation*

VI. On the Rotation of the Letters and the Zodiac

"When we say that it is by means of these media that the Eternal, Master of hosts, God of Israel, Living Elohim, Almighty, Sufficient, Noble and Sublime, Dwelling in Eternity, Holy Be His Name has traced the twenty-two letters according to the construction of the sphere, we refer to the sphere's rotation which displaces to the rear what was positioned to the fore. It is the same with the letters when one inverts them, putting to the rear what had been at the fore. Proof of this is demonstrated when one says 'oneg' ['delight'] which is something desirable, and when one says 'nega' ['plague'] which is something detestable: the letters are the same, only inverted."

This verse is the pivotal point of the book, namely that the Creator - Holy Be His Name - has so disposed some of the letters and numbers to create a kind of body. Later He transposed their positions in order to create a body different from the first. The author gives us two comparisons drawn from the rotation of the sphere and the rotation of the letters. More examples could be adduced, but we will begin with these two. If the three letters : **Het**, **Tsadeh** and **Resh** are combined, their meaning in this order is "courtyard." If we change the position of the **Tsadeh** and **Resh**, pronouncing the word **harats**, its meaning becomes "to cut." If we combine the letters in the order of **Resh**, **Tsadeh** and **Het**, which is pronounced **retsah**, the meaning is changed to 'murder'. If we combine the letters in the order of **Tsadeh**, **Het**, and **Resh**, this is then pronounced **tsohar** and means "whiteness". These four words are examples of the same letters used in different order. Sometimes

Page 143

ספר יצירה

the different ways of combining letters do not have a significance. If the letters **Qof, Shin** and **Resh** are combined in this order, they signify **qashar**, "to bind." If they are recombined in the form of **Qof, Resh** and **Shin**, or **qeresh**, the meaning is "beam." The same letters combined as **sharaq** means "hiss," and the combination of **Resh, Shin** and **Qof** is pronounced reshaq and means "happiness". There is, however, no meaning to the combination of **Resh, Qof** and **Shin** in this language. A word with four letters multiplies the number of possible combinations just as a word with five letters multiplies them even more so [. . .]

. . . It is especially clear to anyone versed in the science of the sphere's revolution. When the sphere turns the measure of one zodiacal sign, diverse figures result which bring a corresponding influence into play, according to the data of this science. Let us examine the represented image of the sphere for this present day, which is Tuesday, the twelfth of Sivan in the year 1242; the Sun was at the 7° of Gemini, the Moon at the 2° of Scorpio, Saturn at the 14° of Capricorn, Jupiter at 25° of Pisces, Mars at 40° of Pisces, Venus at 25° of Cancer, and Mercury at 20° of Taurus. If we begin our work in the first and second hours of the day, the most powerful luminaries in the celestial sphere are the Sun at the horizon and Jupiter and Mars since they are both in the middle of the sky. The four other planets are hidden since Venus is in the 2°, the Moon in the 6°, Saturn in the 8° and Mercury in the 12°. Everything under the influence of the first three is strongly effected because their light falls on the horizon. The influence from the four other planets is weak because the horizon does not receive their light. If we do our work during the third and fourth hours of the day, the celestial sphere has already turned one sign. Cancer is on the horizon, the Moon is at the 5°, Saturn in the 7°, Jupiter and Mars at 9°, Mercury at 11°s. The influence of each of them depends upon its force from its position. If we do our work during the fifth and sixth hours of the day, two signs have turned and Leo is on the horizon. The powerful luminaries in the sphere are the Sun because it is in the 11°, Mercury at 10°, and the Moon at 4°. As for Venus, Saturn, Jupiter and Mars, they are all hidden, and those under their influence will feel their effect. If we conduct our work during the seventh and eighth hours of the day, a quarter of the sphere will have turned, Virgo will be at the horizon and none of the planets will be hidden. The Moon will be at 3°, Saturn at 5°, Jupiter and Mars at 6°, Mercury at 9°, Venus at 11°. In this case, all the influences compliment one another. If we are working in the ninth and tenth hours of the day, one animal of the sphere will have turned. Scorpio will appear along with the Moon, and the sphere will take another form according to its revolution. The influence of the rays, the horoscope and other astronomical conditions are subsequently transformed as the sphere revolves. Fixed stars, changing stars, and stars which have two bodies likewise demonstrate this transformation during each quarter of the day (which begin anew each six hours). I have drawn out these examples only because the author has stressed them by saying: "the sphere turns forwards and backwards."

ספר יצירה

VII. On the Ethereal Realm and its Relation to Prophecy

The Holy Scriptures call the second, more tenuous air **Kavod** ["glory"], as it is said: "the whole earth is full of His glory" [Isaiah VI, 3]; and God Himself has declared: "But as truly as I live, all the earth shall be filled with the glory of the Eternal" [Numbers XIV, 21]. The people call him **Shekhinah** ["dwelling" or "abode"] as it is said: "And the glory of the Eternal abode" [Exodus XXIV, 16], and elsewhere: "that glory may dwell in our land" [Psalms LXXXV, 9]. The author of our book has called Him "breath of the Living God" as it is said: "And my spirit will remain in the midst of thee, that thou fearest not," [Haggai II, 5]. Via this second, tenuous air, the word of prophecy was delivered, as it is said: "The Spirit of the Eternal God is upon me" [Isaiah LXI, 1]. It is also via this second, tenuous air that all the visible miracles appeared to the prophets, as it is said: "in a vision by the Spirit of God" [Ezekiel XI, 24]. This is evidently a created thing, for everything outside the Creator ---may His Name be exalted!---is a created thing, as it is said: "there is none other beside Him" [Deuteronomy IV, 35]. By way of this second, tenuous, but created air, which is in the world as life is in man, the created word heard by Moses in the visible air has been produced along with the decalogue heard by our fathers. This has been called: "voice of the living God" [Deuteronomy V, 26]. Through the voice of the living God, the seven qualifications of the voice of the Eternal were spoken. From this second air comes the knowledge of wisdom, which God bequeaths to distinguished men, as it is said: "And the spirit of the Eternal shall rest upon him, the spirit of wisdom and understanding, the spirit of council..." [Isaiah

ספר יצירה

XI, 2]. From this knowledge come the faculties of courage and bravery, which God grants to whomsoever He will, as it is said: "Then the Spirit of the Eternal came upon Jephthah" [Judges XI, 29] and: "But the Spirit of the Eternal came upon Gideon" [Judges VI, 34]. For this reason, the author of our book has given "life of the worlds" as the first name.

As for the sense of the words: "whose throne is fortified from the beginning," this means that the second, tenuous air is for God --- may He be celebrated and exalted! ---just as the throne, by comparison, is for the king. Thus it is said: "The Eternal hath prepared His throne in the heavens; and His kingdom ruleth over all," [Psalms CIII, 19]. This is the reason why the Tabernacle has been called His throne, according to the verse: "they shall call Jerusalem the throne of the Eternal" [Jeremiah III, 17].

As for the meaning of the words: "blessed and whose name is blessed" this is a general appellation for the light which enters the visible air of the entire world below, as it is said: "And blessed be His glorious name for ever: and let the whole earth be filled with his glory" [Psalms LXXII, 19]. This object is also what the Wise have called "**Ruach Ha-Qodesh**" ["Holy Spirit"]. Actually, after the prophecy had disappeared, a light appeared to them as if it were reflected by a mirror, and they heard a voice like an echo, that is to say that the desert reverberated it to them, and this has been called "**Bath Qol**" ["daughter of the voice"], which means child by the voice. With regard to this, Scripture has said: "And thine ears shall hear a word behind thee, saying. . . ." [Isaiah XXX, 21]. Scripture has not said: ["before thee"].

Sepher Yetzirah   *Book of Creation*

The author of our book says that this concept was the first created thing, and it is the most tenuous thing in existence, but also the strongest. This is followed by the visible air where the Creator has formed the ten numbers and the twenty-two letters. . . .

ספר יצירה

VIII. On the Geometry of Phonetics and the Order of the Alphabet

The twenty-two letters are three principals, seven doubles, and twelve simples, which are cleaved in the air, traced by the voice and situated in five places in the mouth. They have divided themselves into five sections: (1) Alef, He, Het, Ayin are pronounced at the extremity of the tongue with the uvula; (2) Bet, Vav, Mem , Peh are pronounced with the lips touching and with the tip of the tongue; (3) Gimel, Yod, Kaf, Qof are articulated with the side of the tongue; (4) Dalet, Tet, Lamed, Nun, Tav with the middle of the tongue; (5) Zayin, Shin, Samekh, Resh, and Tsadeh are pronounced between the teeth with a quiet tongue [Chapter Four, ¶3].

According to the different locations in the mouth necessary to articulate them, there is also a difference between the letters as they are traced into the air. Thus the author has said "cleaved in the air," "traced by the voice". The voice traces the letters, dispatches them through the air, cleaves and orders them. The group **Alef, He, Het** and **Ayin** [ahacha] is the more delicate and produces a straight line in the air. This is followed by **Gimel, Yod, Kaf** and **Qof** [gikhaq], which produce either unequal or equilateral triangular figures in the air according to their motion. This group is followed by **Dalet, Tet, Lamed, Nun, Tav** [datlanat] which produce square figures, either simple or complex according to their movement. Then follows **Zayin, Shin, Samech, Resh,** and **Tsadeh** [zshosrots] which produce oblique figures, some right angled, others acute or obtuse according to their movement in the air. Finally the letters **Bet, Vav ,**

ספר יצירה

Mem and **Peh** [bumaph] produce spherical forms in the air according to the force of their pronunciation, some being simple and others more complex. The author has enumerated the group [bumaph] after [ahacha] because **Bet** is the second letter of the alphabet. He who first established the alphabetical sequence, situated **Bet** towards the beginning to separate these five different letter groups, and to prevent their combination, as well as to eliminate any difficulties for students and children in pronouncing the letters. Actually, the composition of words with these twenty-two letters usually combines only the letters corresponding to the different vocal organs. Two letters which belong to the same letter grouping are very rarely combined with one another. Thus **Zayin** and **Shin** never appear next to each other in the Hebraic tongue; nor do **Samech** and **Shin**; nor **Kaf** and **Gimel**; nor are **Dalet** and **Tet** coupled in the same word. I have already explained this in the first of the grammatical books. ...

Sepher Yetzirah   *Book of Creation*

IX. On the 231 Gates of Letter Permutation

When He traced, cut, multiplied, weighed and inverted the twenty-two letters, He created everything which has been created, and everything which will be created in the future. How did He multiply them? Aleph [א] with each of the letters and each with Alef, Bet with each one and each one with Bet, and the same for Gimel. He turned and inverted them all, and formed the totality of 231 words. All the creatures and all the words cannot exist without another being above them. [Chapter Four, 4].

I have translated the words "**hozerot halilah**" as "they turn in a circle and invert themselves" because every hollow thing is so called in the Hebrew language. The words "**n'vuv luhot**" ["hollow with boards," Exodus XXVII, 8] are written as "**halil luhin**" in the Targum. Concerning the orifices of the body, it is said that: "God has created in it many holes and cavities" [Berakhot 60 b]. In paraphrase, the Targum has likewise said of the king of Tyre: "But you have not considered your body which has been made with cavities and holes which are indispensible" [paraphrase of Ezekiel XXVIII, 13]. Similarly, the totality of air in the world is called "hollow of the world" because it always revolves [circulates].

This passage is sometimes misunderstood to say: "They are found to exit through two hundred twenty-one gates," and this is incorrect. Though we have learned that calculation demands that this number total two hundred thirty-one, the only number that I have seen written is "two hundred twenty-one." I have no doubt that this is an

ספר יצירה

error. A similar mistake can be found in the **Four Gates**: "every Tishri of an embolismic year which begins before 695 parts of the twelfth hour." Now, in all the texts I have found "the 11th hour" written instead of the twelfth, but this is an error. If you add the surplus of two years, one of which is an embolismic year, the new moon will be at exactly five o'clock on the Sabbath, but it must be at exactly six o'clock. It will not be at six, however, unless the twelfth hour is set as the starting point. Analogously, in response to our author's question, "How did he multiply them," it is correct to give the number two hundred thirty-one as the answer. I will explain this in accordance with the principle which the author himself applies: "**Alef** with all the letters and all with **Alef**, **Bet** with all and all with **Bet**," etc. This kind of multiplication can be found in the cities of Palestine and Egypt. The children write this in order to learn how to spell, and these are the twenty-two series which are called rows [files]. The first row is **Alef-Alef, Alef-Bet, Alef-Gimel, Alef-Dalet, Alef-He, Alef-Vav, Alef-Zayin**, up to **Alef-Tav**. The second row is **Bet-Alef, Bet-Bet, Bet-Gimel, Bet-Dalet, Bet-He, Bet-Vav, Bet-Zayin** up to **Bet-Tav**. The third row is **Gimel-Alef, Gimel-Bet, Gimel-Gimel, Gimel-Dalet, Gimel-He, Gimel-Vav, Gimel-Zayin** up to **Gimel-Tav**. It is the same for **Dalet-Alef, He-Alef**, up to **Tav-Alef, Tav-Bet, Tav-Gimel** etc., up to **Tav-Tav**. In all, this amounts to twenty-two multiplied by twenty-two or four hundred eighty-four. Of this total, twenty-two words must be subtracted which are not products [of one letter with another], namely **Alef-Alef** of the first row, **Bet-Bet** of the second row, **Gimel-Gimel** of the third row, **Dalet-Dalet** of the fourth row, and so on up to **Tav-Tav** of the twenty-second row. The reason for this subtraction is as follows: if **Dalet** is combined with **Dalet**, for example, it simply produces the same figure in the air and a single word in the verse, and they remain in their original state when they are inverted. Once we have subtracted these twenty-two [duplicates], we are left with four hundred sixty-two. Of these four hundred sixty-two, however, only a half are actually different sets of pairs. The pair **Alef-Bet** in the first row is like the pair **Bet-Alef** in the second row; **Alef-Gimel** in the first row is like **Gimel-Alef** in the third; **Alef-Dalet** in the first is like **Dalet-Alef** in the fourth, and so on for each of the series. One therefore discovers that one half of the letters simply reproduces the other half, and thus it is said: "And they all turn in a circle" because they turn into their reverse. When one subtracts half of the four hundred sixty-two, the remainder is two hundred thirty-one. Thus we have said: "The letters are found to exit through two hundred thirty-one gates". A person can make visible sense of this simply by calculating with coins or by writing rows of letters and counting them. This explains how the apparent unity above all multiplication is an index of the One, the Holy, may He be praised and exalted!

I have heard that a commentator on our book has kept the mistake of two hundred twenty-one gates. He has attempted to justify this error by saying that the total of **Alef-Alef**, **Alef-Bet**, **Alef-Gimel**, **Alef-Dalet** and so on is only twenty-one since **Alef-Alef** is not multiplied [combined] and **Alef** revolves only around itself. This commentator then multiplies these twenty-one by ten, i.e., the ten numbers, and this amounts to two hundred ten. Then he adds the ten numbers and **Alef**, which is the first unity, and this amounts to two hundred twenty-one. But ---may God have mercy upon thee---

ספר יצירה

this is a concatenation of a tissue of errors, all due to the fact that the commentator does not know how to multiply. We can cite five reasons why his explanation is in error: (1) he has multiplied **Alef** with all the letters but not all the letters with **Alef**. Later on he repeats this mistake by failing to multiply **Bet** with all or all with **Bet**, and the same with the other letters. He has only multiplied **Alef** with all; (2) he has multiplied the sum of **Alef** with all (i.e., twenty-one) by ten, but there is no reason to multiply by ten. The author of our book has not given this direction. He has only directed the inquirer to multiply the letters, and he says "**Alef** with all" and "**Bet** with all". He has not mentioned the ten numbers in this section. The commentator has thus neglected this direction and has done what was not directed at all; (3) he has separately added the ten numbers to his product, but this is the chapter on multiplication and not abstraction. Were this the chapter on abstraction, one would add the twenty-two isolated letters, and this would then amount to two hundred forty-three; (4) the commentator has omitted the double **Alef** without multiplying it by ten, and therefore must add the isolated **Alef**, but there is no reason for this procedure; (5) this commentator's book also contains the phrase: "and they all turn in a circle." Now if the letters are multiplied one by another, they do turn in a circle, but they do not turn in a circle if they are merely multiplied by ten. With that said, I should like to know what remains of this commentator's argument to be defended.

Our author's purpose in this chapter on multiplication is to demonstrate that the Creator---may He be exalted!---by composing these twenty-two letters through the five procedures of tracing, carving, multiplying, weighing and transposing has created all that has been and will create all that will exist in the future. Actually, when He traced straight lines through the circumferences, triangles in the squares, and drew oblique lines in these circumferences, triangles and squares, the results were surfaces and volumes folding in upon one another according to these marvelous methods which create all forms. This is by the penetration of the **Bet** in the **Gimel**, the **Dalet** in the **He**, etc. For this reason, the pairs **Alef-Alef, Bet-Bet, Gimel-Gimel, Dalet-Dalet** up to **Tav-Tav** do not enter into such multiplication. If you say **Alef** one hundred times, it only results in a single form in the air, namely a straight line. And if you speak **Bet** a hundred times, you will only trace a single circular form repeatedly. This explains the creation of the letter forms in the air. However, we can only establish this form in our spirit. We will not be able to realize this form because it belongs to the Master of the worlds---may He be praised and exalted! The wise, therefore, first teach their students mathematics and geometry, for these are the origin of knowledge. ....[. . .]

ספר יצירה

X. On the Crowning of the Letters

The reference to each letter, "and He attached a crown to it" conforms to an ancient principle---of happy memory! One tradition of the letters is that they have been revealed with ornaments and crowns, as it is said: "Seven letters necessitate three adornments: **Shin, Ayin, Tet, Nun, Zayin, Gimel** and **Tsadeh**" [Menahot 29 b]. It is the same for each letter. For some letters, these adornments augment and for others they restrain the deductions drawn from them, as **The Book of Crowns** has explained. The ancients also had the tradition that when the crowns are not carefully written in the Torah, it is forbidden to pronounce benedictions upon it, and it is not permitted to read it in public. For this reason, they say that one who hastily rushes through it will not live long. The ancient amulet makers say that the letters are worthless if they have not been written with their crowns. Similarly, our author says that it is not possible to form the triangular, square, folded, chain-formed, or convex figures (which the letters were meant to form) without a crown. He says, therefore, that "He attached a crown to it".

ספר יצירה

Sepher Yetzirah   Book of Creation

The Sefer Yetzirah

G. Scholem Translation

ספר יצירה

Sepher Yetzirah   Book of Creation

Chapter 1

1. With 32 wonderous paths of Wisdom engrave Yah, the Lord of Hosts, [God of Israel, the Living God, King of the Universe, Almighty God, merciful and gracious, High and Exalted, dwelling in eternity, whose name is Holy, and create His universe] with three books, with text (Sepher), with number (Sephar), and with communication (Sippur).

2. Ten Sefirot of Nothingness plus twenty two [foundations] letters:

   Three Mothers, Seven Doubles, and Twelve Elementals.

3. Ten Sefirot of Nothingness:

   The number of the ten fingers, five opposite five, with a single covenent precisely in the middle, like the circumcision of the tongue and the circumcision of the membrum.

4. Ten Sefirot of Nothingness:

   Ten and not nine; ten and not eleven. Understand with Wisdom, and be wise with Understanding. Examine with them and probe them, make a thing stand on its essence, and make the Creator sit on his base.

5. Ten Sefirot of Nothingness:

ספר יצירה

Their measure is ten which have no end. A depth of beginning, a depth of end; a depth of good, a depth of evil; a depth of above, a depth below; a depth east, a depth west; a depth north, a depth south. The singular Master, God faithful King, dominates them all from His holy dwelling until eternity of eternities.

6. Ten Sefirot of Nothingness:

   Their vision is like the "appearance of lightening", their limit has no end. His Word in them is "running and returning". They rush to his saying like a whirlwind, and before His throne they prostrate themselves.

7. Ten Sefirot of Nothingness:

   Their end is embedded in their beginning, and their beginning in their end, like a flame in a burning coal. For the Master is singular, He has no second. And before One, what do you count?

8. Ten Sefirot of Nothingness:

   Bridle your mouth from speaking and your heart from thinking. And if your heart runs, return to the place, as it is written, "The Chayot running and returning" (Ezekizl 1:14). Regarding this covenant was made.

9. Ten Sefirot of Nothingness:

Sepher Yetzirah — Book of Creation

One is the Breath of the Living God, blessed and benedicted be the Name of the Life of worlds. Voice, Breath and Speech. This is the Holy Breath (Ruach HaKodesh).

Two: Breath from Breath.

With it engrave and carve twenty-two foundation letters - three, Mothers, seven Doubles, and twelve Elementals - and one Breath is from them.

10. *Three:* Water and Breath.

    With it engrave and carve chaos and void, mire and clay. Engrave them like a garden plot, carve them like a wall, cover them like a ceiling.

11. *Four:* Fire from water.

    With it engrave and carve the Throne of Glory, Seraphim, Ophanim, holy Chayot, and Ministering Angels. From the three establish His dwelling, as it is written, "He makes His angels of breaths, His ministers from flaming fire" (Psalms 104:4).

12. *Five:*

    With three of the simple letters seal "above". Choose three and place them in His great Name: YHV. With them seal the six extremities. Face upward and seal it with YHV.

ספר יצירה

Six:

Seal "below". Face downward and seal it with YHV.

Seven:

Seal "east. Face straight ahead and seal it with HYV.

Eight:

Seal "west". Face backward and seal it with HVY

Nine:

Seal "south". Face to the right and seal it withn VYH.

Ten:

Seal "north". Face to the left and seal it with VHY.

These are the Ten Sefirot of Nothingness. One is the Breath of the Living God. Breath [from Breath], Fire [from water, and the extremities], up, down, east, west, north and south.

Sepher Yetzirah   *Book of Creation*

Chapter 2

1. Twenty-two foundation letters:

three Mothers, seven Doubles, and twelve Elementals. The three Mothers, AMSh, their foundation is the pan of merit, the pan of liability, and the tongue of decree deciding between them.

2. Twenty-two letters:

Engrave them, carve them, weigh them, permute them, and transform them, and with them depict the soul of all that was formed and all that will be formed in the future.

3. Twenty-two foundation letters:

They are engraved with voice, carved with breath, and placed in the mouth in five places: AChHO, BVMP, GYKO, DTLNTh, ZSShRTz.

4. Twenty-two foundation letters:

They are set in a circle as 231 Gates. And this is the sign: There is no good higher than delight (ONG), and there is no evil lower than plague (NGO).

5. How?

ספר יצירה

Weigh them and transpose them, Aleph with each one, and each one with Aleph; Bet with each one, and each one with Bet. They repeat in a cycle. Therefore, everything formed and everything spoken emanates in one name.

> 6. From substance out of chaos and make nonexistence into existence.

Carve great pillars out of air that cannot be grasped.
This is the sign:
One forsees, transposes, and makes all creation and all words with one Name. And a sign of this: Twenty-two objects in a single body.

Chapter 3

1. Three Mothers, AMSh:

Their foundation is the pan of liability, the pan of merit, and the tongue of decree deciding between them.

2. Three Mothers, AMSh:

A great, mystical, concealed secret, sealed with six rings. And from it emanate fire and water, separating themselves as male and female. Three Mothers, AMSh, are their foundation, and from them are born the Fathers, from which everything was created.

3. Three Mothers, AMSh, in the Universe are air, water, and fire.

Heaven was created from fire, earth was created from water, and the air decides decides between the fire and the water.

4. Three Mothers AMSh, in the year are fire, water, and breath.

The hot is created from fire, the cold is created from water, and the temperate from breath decides between them.

5. Three Mothers, AMSh, in the Soul are fire, water, and breath.

ספר יצירה

The head is created from fire, the belly is created from water, and the chest, created from breath, decides between them.

6. Three Mothers, AMSh:

Engrave them, carve them, permute them, and with them seal three Mothers in the Universe, three Mothers in the Year, and three Mothers in the Soul, male and female.

7. Make aleph king over breath,

bind a crown to it, and combine one with another. And with them seal air in the Universe, the temperate in the year, and the chest in the Soul, the male with AMSh, and the female with AShM.

8. Make Mem king over water, bind a crown to it, and combine one with another.

And with them seal earth in the Universe, the cold in the Year, and the belly in the Soul, the male with MASh, and the female with ShMA.

Chapter 4

1. Seven Doubles, BGD KPRT:

Their foundation is life, peace, wisdom, wealth, grace, seed, dominnance. Each has two sounds: B-Bh, G-Gh, D-Dh, K-Kh, P-Ph, R-Rh, T-Th. Astructure of soft and hard, a structure of strong and weak, double because they are transposes. The transpose of life is death, the transpose of peace is evil, the transpose of wisdom is folly, the transpose of wealth is poverty, the transpose of grrace is is ugliness, the transpose of seed is desolation, the transpose of dominance is subjugation.

2. Seven Doubles, BGD KPRT: Seven and not six, seven and not eight.

Examine with them and probe from them, make each thing stand on its own essence, and make the Creator sit on His base.

3. Seven Doubles, BGD KPRT, parallel the seven extremeties.

These are the six extremeties: up, down, east, west, north, south. And the Holy Palace precisely in the middle upholds them all.

4. Seven Doubles, BGD KPRT: Engrave them,

ספר יצירה

carve them, combine them, as planets in the Universe, days in the Year, and gates in the Soul.

From them engrave seven firmaments, seven earths, seven weeks. Seven is therefore beloved under all heavens.

5. How?

Make Bet king over life, bind a crown to it, and with it depict Saturn in the universe, Sunday in the Year, and the right eye in the Soul.

6. Make Gimel king, bind a crown to it,

and with it depict Jupiter in the Universe, Monday in the Year, and the left eye in the Soul.

7. Make Dalet king, bind a crown to it,

and with it depict Mars in the Universe, Tuesday in the Year, and the right ear in the Soul.

8. Make Kaf king, bind a crown to it,

and with it depict the Sun in the Universe, Wedneday in the Year, and the left ear in the Soul.

9. Make Peh king, bind a crown to it,

and with it depict Venus in the Universe, Thursday in the Year, and the right nostril in the Soul.

10. Make Resh king, bind a crown to it,

and with it depict Mercury in the Universe, Friday in the Year, and the left nostril in the Soul.

11. Make Tav king, bind a crown to it,

and with it depict the Moon in the Universe, the Sabbath in the Year, and the mouth in the Soul.

12. The Seven Doubles, how does one permute them?

Two stones build two houses, three build six houses, four build 24 houses, five build 120 houses, six build 720 houses, and seven build 5040 houses. From there on go out and calculate that which the mouth cannot speak and the ear cannot hear.

These are the seven planets in the Universe: The Sun, Venus, Mercury, the Moon, Saturn, Jupiter, Mars.

These are the seven days in the Year: The seven days of creation. And the seven gates in the Soul are the two eyes, the two ears, the two nostrils, and the mouth. And with them were engraves the seven firmaments, the seven earths, the seven hours.

ספר יצירה
Seven is therefore beloved for every desire under heaven.

Chapter 5

1. Twelve Elementals: HV ZCh TY LN SO TzQ.

    Their foundation is sight, hearing, smell, speech, taste, coition, action, motion, anger, laughter, thought, and sleep. Their measure is the twelve diagonal boundaries: the north-east boundary, the south-east boundary, the upper-east boundary, the lower-east boundary, the upper-north boundary, the lower-north boundary, the south-west boundary, the north-west boundary, the upper-west boundary, the lower-west boundary, the upper-south boundary, the lower-south boundary. They continually spread for ever and ever. They are the Arms of the Universe.

2. Twelve Elementals: HV ZCh TY LN SO TzQ.

    Engrave them, carve them weigh them, permute them, transpose them, and with them depict the twelve constellations in the Universe: Aries, Taurus, Gemini. Cancer, Leo, Virgo, Libra, Scorpio, Sagittarius, Capricorn, Aquarius, and Pisces; the twelve months in the Year: Nissan, Iyar, Sivan, Tamuz, Av, Elul, Tishrei, Mar-cheshvan, Kislev, Tevet, Shevat, Adar; and the twelve directors of the Soul: two hands, two feet, two kidneys, the spleen, the liver, the gall bladder, the hemsess, the kiva, and the korkeban.

ספר יצירה

How does one permute them? Make Heh king, bind a crown in it, and with it depict Aries in the Universe, Nissan in the Year, and the right hand in the Soul. Make Vav king, bind a crown to it, and with it depict Taurus, Iyar in the Year, and the left hand in the Soul. Make Zayin king, bind a crown to it, and with it depict Taurus in the Universe, Sivan in the Year, and the right foot in the Soul. Make Chet king, bind a crown to it, and with it depict Cancer in the Universe, Tamuz in the Year, and the left foot in the Soul. Make Tet king, bind a crown to it, and with it depict Leo in the Universe, Av in the Year, and the right kidney in the Soul. Make Yud king, bind a crown to it, and with it depict Virgo in the Universe, Elul in the Year, and the left kidney in the Soul. Make Lamed king, bind a crown to it, and with it depivt Libra in the Universe, Tishrei in the Year, and the liver in the Soul. Make Nun king, bind a crown to it, and with it depict Scorpio in the Universe, Mar-cheshvan in the Year, and the spleen in the Soul. Make Samekh kin, bind a crown to it, and with it depict Sagittarius in the Universe, Kislev in the Year, and the gall bladder in the Soul. Make Eyin king, bind a crown to it, and with it depict Capricorn in the Universe, Tevet in the Year, and the hemsess in the Soul. Make Tzadi king, bind a crown to it, and with it depict Aquarius in the Universe, Shevat in the Year, and the kivah in the Soul. Make Kuf king, bind a crown to it, and with it depict Pisces in the Universe, Adar in the Year, and the korkeban in the Soul.

3. Three Mothers which are three Fathers,

   from which emanate fire, breath and water. Three Mothers, seven Doubles, and twelve Elementals.

4. These are the twenty-two letters which are founded by the Blessed Holy One

   [Yah, YHVH of Hosts, God of Israel, the Living God, high and exalted] dwelling in eternity, whose name is Holy, exalted and Holy is He.

ספר יצירה

Sepher Yetzirah   Book of Creation

Chapter 6

1. Three are the fathers and their offspring, seven are the planets and their hosts, and twelve are the diagonal boundaries.

    And the proof of this, true witnesses, are the Universe, the Year, and the Soul. He decreed Twelve, (Ten), Seven and Three and He appointed them in the Teli, the Cycle, and the Heart. The three are fire, water, and breath: fire above, water below, and breath, the decree that decides between them. A sign of this is that fire upholds water. Mem hums, Shin hisses, and Alef is the decree that decides between them.

2. The Teli in the Universe is like a king on his throne, the cycle in the Year is like a king in the province, the Heart in the Soul is like a king in battle.

    "Also every desire, one opposite the other was made by God" (ecclesiastes 7:14). Good opposite evil, good from good, evil from evil. Good makes evil recognizable, and evil makes good recognizable. Good is kept for the good, and evil is kept for the wicked.

3. Three: Each one stands alone.

    Seven are divided, three opposite three, with a decree deciding between them. Twelve stand in war: three

ספר יצירה

who love, three who hate, three who give life, and three who kill. The three that love are the heart, the ears and the mouth; the three that hate are the liver. the gall bladder, and the tongue. And God, the faithful King dominates them all. One over three, three over seven, and seven over twelve, and all of them are bound, one to another.

4. And when Abraham our father gazed, he looked, saw, delved, understood, engraved, carved, permuted and depicted, and he was successful.

And the Master of all, Blessed be He, revealed Himself to him, and took him in His bosom, [kissed him on the head, and called him, "my Beloved"]. He made a covenant with him between the ten toes of his feet-this is the covenant of circumcision-and between the ten fingers of his hand-this is the covenant of the tongue. He bound the twenty-two letters to his tongue and revealed their foundation. He drew them in water, burned them in fire, agitated them with breath. He ignited them with seven planets, and directed them with twelve constellations.

Sepher Yetzirah   Book of Creation

THE SEPHER YETZIRAH
Heidrick Translation

The Book of Creation

Translation by Bill Heidrick

An adapted but complete version based on the Kalisch and Akiba-Stenring translations - with adjusted correspondences to conform with the researches of the Order of the Golden Dawn.

Declared in manuscript to be forever in the public domain - June, 1976 e.v.

Adaptation and parenthetic notes.

Adapted to conform to the Golden Dawn correspondences in 1976 e.v. with parenthetic notes by Bill Heidrick from the Kalisch and Stenring translations. This rendering of the S.Y. is made in the public domain as a way of paying dues of another kind. The notes are in curly brackets: {}, and are not part of the original text. The "Sepher Yetzirah" is the ultimate basis of the Golden Dawn system of correspondences embodied in Crowley's "Liber 777".]

The "Sepher Yetzirah" is one of the most important founding works of Qabalah. It was composed probably between the 3rd and 6th centuries of the Christian era and was later attributed to R. Akiba. For more information on the history of this work, see Gershom Scholem's "Kabbalah", Quadrangle/The New York Times Book Co., 1974. Scholem's work is essential for students of Qabalah, but must be taken with considerable skepticism in its conclusions.

ספר יצירה

Sepher Yetzirah *Book of Creation*

Chapter One

Section One

Yah, Jehovah of hosts, the living Elohim, King of the Universe, Omnipotent, All-King and Merciful, Supreme and Extolled, Who is Eternal, Sublime and Most -Holy, formed and created the Universe in thirty-two mysterious paths of wisdom by three Sepharim, namely: Sfor, Sippur and Sapher {Samekh-Peh-Resh, Samekh-Peh-Vau-Resh and Samekh-Peh-Resh: These angelic names mean: Numbers, Letters and Words} which are in Him one and the same. They consist of ten Sephiroth out of nothing and of twenty-two fundamental letters. He divided the twenty-two consonants into three divisions: Three Mothers, fundamental letters or first elements; Seven Double; and Twelve Simple consonants.

Section Two

The ten Sephiroth out of nothing is analogous to that of the ten fingers {and toes} of the human body, five parallel to five, and in the center of which is the covenant with the only One {between the hands this is the tongue. Between the feet this is the circumcised penis or the broken hymen} by the word of the tongue and the rite of Abraham.

Section Three

Ten are the Sephiroth {often translated as "numbers", this word has no English true equivalent} out of nothing, and not the number

ספר יצירה

nine, ten and not eleven. Comprehend this great wisdom, understand {Chokmah and Binah in the text} this knowledge, inquire into it and ponder on it, render it evident and lead the Creator back to His throne again {In other words, descend the Tree of Life to learn Ma'aseh Berishit and ascend it to accomplish the goal of Ma'aseh Merkabah.}

Section Four

The Ten Sephiroth out of nothing are infinite in ten ways: The beginning infinite {Kether}; The end infinite {Chokmah}; The good infinite {Binah}; The evil infinite {Chesed}; The height infinite {Geburah}; The depth infinite {Tiphireth}; The East infinite {Netzach}; The West infinite {Hod}; The North infinite {Yesod}; The South infinite {Malkuth} - {These last four are given in a different order in some versions.}, and the only Lord God, the faithful King, rules over all from His holy habitation for ever and ever.

Section Five

The appearance of the Sephiroth out of nothing is like a flash of lightning, being without end, His word is in them, when they go and return; they run by His order like a whirlwind and humble themselves before His throne {The divine names of the lightning bolt are: Eheieh, Yah, Yahweh Elohim, El, Elohim Gibor, Jehovah Eloh Va-Da'at, Jehovah Tzabaoth, Elohim Tzabaoth, Shadi El Chi, Adoni Melekh Ha-Aretz.}

Section Six

The Sephiroth out of nothing has its end linked to its beginning and its beginning linked to its end, just as the flame is wedded to the live coal; because the Lord is one and there is not a second one, and before one what will you count {"count" has the suggestion meaning of "consider a Sephira."}?

Section Seven

Concerning the number ten of the Sephiroth out of nothing, keep your tongue from speaking and your mind from pondering it and if your mouth urges you to speak and your heart to think about it, return {from questioning the number ten of them}! as it reads: "And the living creatures ran and returned," {Ezekiel: I, 14} and upon this {Mystery} was the covenant made.

Section Eight

These are the ten Sephiroth out of nothing:

One; The Spirit of the living God {Ruach Elohim Chiim}, praised and glorified be the name {schem} of Him who lives to all eternity. The articulate word of creative power, the spirit and the word are what we call the holy spirit.

Two; Air emanated from the spirit by which He formed and established twenty-two consonants fundamentally. Three of them

ספר יצירה

are truly fundamental letters, or mothers, seven are double and twelve are simple consonants; hence the spirit is the first one.

Three; Primitive water emanated from the air. He formed and established by it Bohu {the more substantial part of Chaos, or the waters below the upper waters of Genesis} mud and loam, made them like a bed, put them up like a wall, and surrounded them as with a rampart, put coldness upon them and they became dust, as it reads; "He says to the coldness {snow} be thou earth." {Job: XXXVI; 6}

Four; Fire or Aether emanated from the water. He established by it the throne of glory, the Seraphim and Opanim, the holy living creatures and the angels, and of these three He formed His habitation, as it reads "Who made His angels spirits, His ministers a flaming fire." {Psalm CIV, 4} He selected three consonants from the simple ones which are in the hidden secret of three mothers or first elements: Aleph -- Air, Mem -- Water, and Shin -- Aether or Fire. He sealed them with spirit and fastened them to His great name {Schem, which can be spelled Shin-Aleph-Memfinal} and sealed with it six dimensions.

Five; He sealed the height and turned towards above. The seal was Yod-Heh-Vau {through Aleph}

Six; He sealed the depth, and turned toward below. The seal was Heh-Yod-Vau {through Aleph}

Seven; He sealed the East and turned forward. The seal was Vau-Yod-Heh {through Mem}

Eight; He sealed the West and turned backward. The seal was Vau-Heh-Yod {through Mem}

Nine; He sealed the {North} and turned to the {left}. The seal was Heh-Vau-Yod {through Shin}

Ten; He sealed the {South} and turned to the {right}. The seal was Yod-Vau-Heh {through Shin}

{Extended note: The letters of the six seals are in different order in different versions of the manuscripts. There is also confusion about the order of South and North, right and left. The latter problem may depend on the divinity having right and left sides opposite to the human right and left. The former problem follows from the latter. Also, the oral tradition that ascribes the passage of the seals through the three Mother letters depends on numbers 2 through 4 of this section.}

Section Nine

These are the ten spheres of existence out of nothing. From the spirit of the living God emanated air, from the air, water, from the water, fire or aether, from the aether, the height and the depth, the East and the West, the North and the South.

ספר יצירה

{Extended Note: This is not a simple system of a single emanation. The Hindu theory of the three Gunas is closer to this than the Neoplatonic theory. Here we have a primary emanation from the three abstract qualities of numbers, letters and words (Sec. 1). The ten sephiroth are emanated in more than three spatial dimensions and interact with the letters via a complex relationship to the three Mother letters. Even the relationship of the three Mother letters to the other letters and to the ten sephiroth is not simple but compound. The higher form of the Mothers has the sequence Aleph then Mem then Shin. From Shin this sequence replicates in a lower form. As we will see in the next chapter, these three Mother letters then take a different order to produce yet a still lower form of the Tree of the Ten Sephiroth. The turning point is described in section eight through permutation of the letters of the name Yah -- as foretold in the first section of this chapter. The order of the three Mother letters given in this chapter is that of the "Cube of Space". The order of these Mother letters given in the next chapter defines a different kind of universe, that of the "Schem" or G.'. D.'. Tree of Life. These two universes (and others hinted at in this first chapter) are considered to be "one above the other" in the sense of abstraction being above the concrete.}

Sepher Yetzirah   *Book of Creation*

Chapter Two

Section One

There are twenty-two letters fundamentally. Three of them are the first elements, true fundamentals or mothers, seven are double and twelve are simple consonants. The three fundamental letters Aleph-Mem-Shin have as their basis the balance. In one scale is the merit and in the other the fault, which are placed in equilibrium by the tongue {This is shown in the Egyptian Book of the Dead as the Weighing of the Soul of the Dead and the Testing of the Balance by Thoth, the god of letters}. The three fundamental letters, Aleph, Mem, Shin, signify, as Mem is mute like the water and Shin hissing like the fire, there is Aleph among them, a breath of air which reconciles them. {The sounds of these three letters resemble the characteristic sounds of their elements: Mem is like the rolling of waves, Shin is Like the hissing of flames and Aleph is like the blowing of the wind.}

Section Two

These are the twenty-two letters which form the foundation {Yod-Samekh-Vau-Dalet, the name later applied to the ninth Sephira, is the word used here in the text.}, after having been appointed and established. He combined, weighed {assigned values} and exchanged them, and formed by them all beings which are in existence, and all these which will be formed in all time to come.

ספר יצירה

Section Three

He established twenty-two letters fundamentally by the voice, formed by the breath of air and fixed them on five places in the human mouth, namely: One at the throat {guttural sounds}, Aleph, Hay, Chet, Ayin. Two at the palate {palatal sounds}, Gimel, Yod, Kaf, Qof. Three, at the tongue {lingual sounds}, Dalet, Tet, Lamed, Nun, Taw. Four, at the teeth {dental sounds}, Zain, Shin, Samekh, Resh, Tzaddi. Five, at the lips {labial sounds}, Bet, Vau, Mem, Peh.

Section Four

He fixed the twenty-two Letters of foundation on the sphere like a wall with 231 gates, and turned the spheres forward and backward. For an illustration may serve the three letters, Gemel, Nun, Ayin. There is nothing better than joy {spelled Ayin-Nun-Gemel in Hebrew} and nothing worse than sorrow or plague {spelled Nun-Gemel-Ayin, in Hebrew. Thus various combinations of the same letters in this language can produce opposite meanings. This is a part of the mysticism of the letters, and also a part of the nature of Hebrew root word formations}

Sepher Yetzirah   *Book of Creation*

Here is one traditional way of presenting the 231:

AB AG AD AH AV AZ ACh AT AY AK AL AM AN AS Aa'a AP ATz AQ AR ASh ATh
BG BD BH BV BZ BCh BT BY BK BL BM BN BS Ba'a BP BTz BQ BR BSh BTh
GD GH GV GZ GCh GT GY GK GL GM GN GS Ga'a GP GTz GQ GR GSh GTh
DH DV DZ DCh DT DY DK DL DM DN DS Da'a DP DTz DQ DR DSh DTh
HV HZ HCh HT HY HK HL HM HN HS Ha'a HP HTz HQ HR HSh HTh
VZ VCh VT VY VK VL VM VN VS Va'a VP VTz VQ VR VSh VTh
ZCh ZT ZY ZK ZL ZM ZN ZS Za'a ZP ZTz ZQ ZR ZSh ZTh
ChT ChY ChK ChL ChM ChN ChS Cha'a ChP ChTz ChQ ChR ChSh ChTh
TY TK TL TM TN TS Ta'a TP TTz TQ TR TSh TTh
YK YL YM YN YS Ya'a YP YTz YQ YR YSh YTh
KL KM KN KS Ka'a KP KTz KQ KR KSh KTh
LM LN LS La'a LP LTz LQ LR LSh LTh
MN MS Ma'a MP MTz MQ MR MSh MTh
NS Na'a NP NTz NQ NR NSh NTh
Sa'a SP STz SQ SR SSh STh
a'aP a'aTz a'aQ a'aR a'aSh a'aTh
PTz PQ PR PSh PTh
TzQ TzR TzSh TzTh
QR QSh QTh
RSh RTh
ShTh

Section Five

But how was it done? He combined, weighed and exchanged: the Aleph with all the other letters in succession, and all the others again with Aleph; Bet with all, and all again with Bet; and so the whole series of Letters {was paired off in very possible way}. Hence it follows that there are 231 formations, and that every creature and every word emanated from one name.

{Extended Note: There are only 231 ways to combine the 22 Hebrew letters into different pairs. The one name is Schem,

ספר יצירה

composed of the three Mother letters Shin, Aleph, and Mem, which provide the basis for all sounds. Schem is the Hebrew word for "Name" especially "Name of the divinity." Schem is usually spelled Shin-Mem, but Aleph can be added to the middle of the word without making a difference in its pronunciation.}

Section Six

He created a reality out of nothing, called the non-existing into existence and shaped colossal pillars from intangible air. This has been shown by the example of combining the letter Aleph with all the other letters, and all the other letters with Aleph. {Of the three Mother Letters, Aleph is the most basic. It's number value is One; and Aleph is the breath of sound carrying air that is necessary to pronounce any and all of the other letters. Thus, the gates of Aleph, the combinations formed between Aleph and all the remaining 21 letters produce the actual sounds of the letters of the Hebrew Alphabet. The pairs or gates with Aleph ARE the spoken Hebrew letters.} He predetermined, and by speaking created every creature and every word by one name. For a sign of this may serve the twenty-two elementary substances {Alphabet letters} by the primitive substance of Aleph.

Sepher Yetzirah *Book of Creation*

Chapter Three

Section One

The three first elements, Aleph Mem Shin, are typified by a balance, in one scale the merit and in the other the fault, which are placed in equilibrium by the tongue. These three mothers, Aleph Mem Shin, are a great, wonderful and unknown mystery, and are sealed by six rings, or elementary circles, namely: air, water, and fire emanated from them, which gave birth again to some offspring {These rings are the ways of ordering three letters, as: Aleph-Mem-Shin, male; Shin-Mem-Aleph, female; Shin-Aleph-Mem, male; Mem-Aleph-Shin, female; Mem-Shin -Aleph, male; Aleph-Shin-Mem, female}

Section Two

God appointed and established the three mothers; combined, weighed and exchanged them, and formed by them three mothers Mem Aleph Shin in the world {the six directions: Above, East and South are probably Male in this tradition. Below, West and North are probably Female in this tradition -- this is the key to the seals of the directions.}, in the year {The six warm months are female two by two while the six cold months are male two by two} and in man, male and female {Here the first rings apply to childhood, the third and fourth to adulthood and the last rings to age}.

Section Three

ספר יצירה

The three mothers Aleph-Mem-Shin in the world are: air, water and fire. Heaven was created from fire or ether {"heaven" or "schemim" starts with the letter Shin in Hebrew}; the earth {comprising sea above land -- "Mem" is both the name of Mem and the Hebrew word for sea} from the elementary water; and the atmospheric air from the elementary air, or spirit, which establishes the balance among them.

Section Four

The three mothers Aleph-Mem-Shin produce in the year heat, coldness and moistness. Heat was created from fire, coldness from water, and moistness from air which equalizes them {fire + water = steam or moist air: Shin + Mem = Aleph, in this particular mystical sense}.

```
   {          1
          3  /  2
           \ / /
           \AAAAAAAAA

              5\        /4
                \      /
                 \ 6 /
                8/    \ 7

 9
 |
                  / AAA \
                 |10    |
                  AAAAA            }
```

Section Five

The three mothers Aleph-Mem-Shin produce in man, male and female, breast, body and head. The head was created from fire {Shin, on the Tree of Life. The upper three Sephiroth are the three prongs of the letter Shin, while the base of the letter forms the Abyss, Aleph-Bet-Dalet-Heh.}, the (belly) from water {Mem, on the Tree of Life. The upper stroke of this letter is the Sephira Yesod -- which is spelled with Yod as its first letter in Hebrew -- and the body of this letter Mem is the Sephira Malkuth -- the Hebrew word "Malkuth" starts with the letter "Mem". In other words, Mem forms the two lowest Sephiroth.}, and the (breast in man, male and female {Aleph, on the Tree of Life forms the middle five Sephiroth by its upper two points, its lower two points and the intersection in the middle of the letter Aleph}) --> (Note: The text of Section Five is corrupt. It has here been "corrected" by comparison to sections six, seven and eight as well as an application of the "theory of cyclic permutation" from the modern mathematics of Group Theory.}

Section Six

First Division. He let the letter Aleph predominate in primitive air, crowned it {made it the top letter of the column in the middle of the Tree of Life. Descending the Tree of Life, the order of the three letters is Aleph, Mem and Shin (male) in Kether, Tiphereth and Yesod. The female order, Shin, Mem and Aleph is encountered by rising up the middle pillar of the Tree and thereby reversing this order.}, combining one with the other and formed by them the air in the world, moistness in the year, and the breast in man, male and female: in male by Aleph-Mem-Shin and in female by Shin-Mem-

ספר יצירה

Aleph {Text corrected by Group Theory -- see note on Section Five. Note also that the breast is the place of the lungs.}

Section Seven

Second Division. He let the letter Mem predominate in primitive water, and crowned it, combined one with the other {made Mem the top letter of the column of Mercy on the right side of the Tree of Life. The order of the three letters is Mem, Shin and Aleph in the Sephiroth Chokmah, Chesed and Netzach {a male ring} going down, and the opposite order {female ring going up. This symbolically makes the pillar of Mercy Male as viewed from the bottom and female as viewed from the top -- there is another way of considering it predominantly male -- by application of the letters of the name Jehovah or Yahweh to the Tree.}, and formed by them the earth {with water over land} coldness in the year, and the belly in male and female; in male by Mem-Shin-Aleph, in female by Aleph-Mem-Shin. {Note that the belly in the human body holds most of the free water of the body.}

Section Eight

Third Division. He let the letter Shin predominate in primitive fire, crowned it, combined one with the other {made Shin the top of the column of severity on the Tree of Life. The order of these three letters is Shin, Aleph, Mem in the Sephiroth Binah, Geburah and Hod going down (Male ring) and Mem, Aleph, Shin going up (Female ring). This makes the pillar of Severity, the left column of the Tree of Life, Male when viewed from the top and Female when viewed from the bottom. By the method of placing Tetragrammaton on the Tree of Life this column is considered predominantly Female}, and formed by them, heaven in the world, heat in the year, and the head of male and female {As a Hebrew word, the name of the letter Shin means "tooth"; and of course the teeth are to be found in the head}.

ספר יצירה

Sepher Yetzirah   *Book of Creation*

Chapter Four

Section One

The seven double letters, Bet Gemel Dalet Koph Peh Resh Taw with a duplicity of pronunciation, aspirated {with a strong outward breath} and unaspirated {without a strong outward breath. These two modes of pronunciation are represented by the presence or absence of a dot in some forms of written and printed Hebrew, the dot or point being called Dagash and placed in the center of the letter} serve as a model of softness and hardness, strength and weakness

{At the time of the writing of the "Sepher Yetzirah" these seven letters were pronounced each in two ways: with outrush of air or with inward sound. They are models for opposite qualities and for the seven planets with their benign and malignant effects. Modern scholars differ as to which of the Hebrew letters originally had this double quality of pronunciation, Mordell holds that a form of Hebrew much older than the writing of the "Yetzirah" had a different usage of this double pronunciation. He has accordingly attempted to reconstruct a "more ancient" version of the "Yetzirh" {See Bibliography}. Modern Hebrew dialects retain a few of these double pronunciations and add new ones.}

Section Two

סםפר יצירה

Seven double letters, Bet Gemel Dalet Koph Peh Resh Taw shall, as it were symbolize Life, Peace, Wisdom, Wealth, Beauty, Fruitfulness and Dominion {Note: this is the list according to the researches of the G.'. D.'.. The qualities are those listed in the "Sepher Yetzirah", but the order of the list is different. The same is true for associations to the seven planets -- for a comparison of the several orderings for these seven Double Letters which are to be found in the different versions of the "Yetzirah", see the Stenring translation noted in the Bibliography}.

Section Three

Seven double letters serve to signify the antithesis to which human life is exposed. The antithesis of Life is Death; of Peace, Strife or War; of Wisdom, Folly; of Wealth, Poverty; of Beauty, Ugliness; of Fruitfulness, Sterility or Childlessness; and of Dominion, Dependence or Slavery.

Section Four

The seven double consonants are analogous to the six dimensions: height and depth {Bet for Above, Gemel for Below}, East and West {Dalet for East, Koph for West}, North and South {Peh for North, Resh for South} and the holy temple that stands in the center {Taw}, which carries them all.

Section Five

Sepher Yetzirah   Book of Creation

The double consonants are seven, Bet Gemel Dalet Koph Peh Resh Taw and not six, they are seven and not eight; reflect upon this fact, inquire about it, and make it so evident, that the Creator be acknowledged to be on His throne again.

{Although this particular statement is often taken as a slap against the speculations of the Gnostics, who were very much at the peak of their activity at the time in which the "Sepher Yetzirah" was written, there are other meanings. If the seven double letters are assigned to the lower seven Sephiroth of the Tree of Life, this may be an injunction to study the fifty gates of understanding; which are the meditations of each of the lower Sephiroth taken as containing divisions corresponding to all the lower seven Sephiroth -- seven times seven or forty-nine plus one, the fiftieth, to refer to the throne of the three higher Sephiroth. Alternately, this may be an injunction to meditate on the spatial or other configurations of these letters as a means of attaining a vision of the letter Taw as the throne of the Creator.}.

Section Six

The seven double consonants, fundamentally, having been designed and established, combined, weighed, and changed by God, He formed by them: seven planets in the world, seven days in the year, seven gates, openings of the senses, in man male and female.

Section Seven

ספר יצירה

The seven planets in the world are: Saturn {Taw}, Jupiter {Koph}, Mars {Peh}, Sun {Resh}, Venus {Dalet}, Mercury {Bet}, Moon {Gemel}. Seven days in the year are the seven days of the week {Sunday, Resh; Monday Gemel; Tuesday, Peh; Wednesday, Bet; Thursday, Koph; Friday, Dalet; and Saturday, Taw}; seven gates in man, male and female are: two eyes, two ears, two nostrils and the mouth

{These applications of the planets to the double letters are the most highly corrupted matter in existing manuscripts of the "Sepher Yetzirah", as is noted further below. No definitive text exists in this matter. The attribution to the seven gates in man, male and female might be as follows: right eye, Bet; left eye, Gemel; right nostril, Peh; left nostril, Resh; right ear, Dalet; left ear, Koph; mouth, Taw. Although this seems reasonable, no certainty is claimed; the allocation suggested here to the human gates is merely plausible. The allocation to the planets is that used by the G.'. D.'. and by the older Thelemic Orders. This allocation to the gates is offered as one alternative to that below.

Section Eight

First Division. He let the letter Bet predominate in Life, crowned it, combined one with the other and formed by them: Mercury in the world, the Fourth day in the year, and the right eye in man, male and female {Contrary to the G.'. D.'. interpretation used here, the more reliable texts say: Moon, First Day and right eye}.

Section Nine

Second Division. He let the letter Gemel predominate in Peace, crowned it, combined one with the other, and formed by them: the Moon in the world, the Second day in the year and right ear in man, male and female.

{There are various associations of the seven gates of the senses to different things. The whole matter is the subject of a tract in the "Sepher Zohar" "The Book of Concealed Mystery" -- this tract may be found in Mather's "Kabbalah Unveiled" and in Luzzatto's "General Principles of the Kabbalah". Neither of these two books provide an exact solution to the allocation of the seven double letters, but they provide material from which the problem may be attacked. The more reliable texts here assign: Mars, Second day and right ear.}

Section Ten

Third Division. He let the letter Dalet predominate in Wisdom, crowned it, combined one with the other, and formed by them: Venus in the world, the sixth day in the year, the right nostril in man, male and female.

{The word translated there as "Man" is actually "Nepesh", the name of the "animal soul" or that which animates the body during life. This word is used in all statements like this one throughout the "Yetzirah" in the Hebrew text. Later mystical traditions ascribe the Nepesh soul to be the ghostly spirit that lingers after death in some cases while higher souls are said to ascend to better places. The more reliable texts here assign: Sun, Third day and right nostril.}

ספר יצירה

Section Eleven

Fourth Division. He let the letter Koph predominate in Wealth, crowned it, combined one with the other, and formed by them: Jupiter in the world, the Fifth day in the year, and the left eye in man, male and female {The more reliable texts here assign: Venus, Fourth day, left eye}.

Section Twelve

Fifth Division. He let the letter Peh predominate in Beauty, crowned it, combined one with the other, and formed by them: Mars in the world, the Third day in the year, and the left ear in man, male and female. {The more reliable texts say: Mercury, Fifth day, left ear}.

Section Thirteen

Sixth Division. He let the letter Resh predominate in Fruitfulness, crowned it, combined one with the other, and formed by them: The Sun in the world, the First day in the year, and the left nostril in man, male and female. {The more reliable texts say: Saturn, Sixth day and left nostril.}

Section Fourteen

Seventh Division. He let the letter Taw predominate in Dominion, crowned it, combined one with the other, and formed by them Saturn in the world, the Seventh day in the year, and the mouth of man, male and female. {The more reliable texts say: Jupiter, Seventh day and mouth.}

Section Fifteen

By the seven double consonants, Bet-Gemel-Dalet-Koph-Peh-Resh-Taw were also designed seven worlds {The lower seven Sephiroth}, seven Heavens {Not the same as the lower seven Sephiroth. The seven Heavens combine certain Sephiroth. They are: Malkut-Yesod, Tipheret; Hod; Netzach; Geburah; Chesed; Da'at-Binah; Chokmah; Keter, -- These are also not to be confused with the seven body centers or Chakras which are variously made to combine to the Sephiroth, most especially in this order: Malkut; Yesod; Hod-Netzach; Tipheret; Geburah-Chesed; Binah-Chokmah; Keter. This latter correspondence is an artificial one, for it breaks down at the Vishuddah, where a complex interaction involves several groups of Sephiroth, including Da'ath, in succession.} seven lands, seven seas, seven rivers, seven deserts, seven days in a week, seven weeks from Passover to Pentecost, there is a cycle, of seven years (widely used in Astrology under various names; e.g. the Saturn Return or Lunation Cycle about 28 years from birth. This country (U.S.A.) has laws based on the seven-fold cycle: legal age at 21, the President must be 35 or older}, the seventh is the release year {In the U.S.A. legal records and statuary limits on some crimes are retained for seven years}, and after seven release years is Jubilee {Fiftieth anniversary is still considered significant in our traditions}. Hence, God loves the number seven under the whole heaven {The theory of seven rays that is popular with Theosophists is based on this seven business. M. Blavatsky probably was greatly

ספר יצירה

influenced by this source, as she was by the "Zohar" in her forgery of the "Seven Stanzas from the Book of Dzyan."}

Section Sixteen

Two stones build two houses {There are only two ways to combine two different letters}, three stones build six houses {the "six rings" of three different letters exhaust the possibilities for three different objects taken three at a time}, four build 24 houses, five build 120 houses, six build 720 houses and seven build 5,040. From thence further go and reckon what the mouth cannot express and the ear cannot hear. {This section outlines the power of combinations of magical powers of the letters and generally spaces out. The manuscripts here prove their corruption through various different errors in the numbers cited. The lost original probably had the combinatorial values correctly stated, as they are given in this edition).

Sepher Yetzirah   *Book of Creation*

Chapter Five

Section One

The twelve simple letters HB:Heh, Vau, Zain, Chet, Tet, Yod, Lamed, Nun, Samekh, Ayin, Tzaddi & Qof symbolize, as it were, the organs of sight, hearing, smell, speech, digestion or swallowing, touch or coition, work, walking, anger, mirth, thinking or meditation, sleep* {The Golden Dawn changed these qualities around quite a bit in disregard of a relatively uniform version in the manuscripts of the SEPHER YETZIRAH. In the following sections, the Golden Dawn term will be given first and then a version from the Kalisch translation: e.g. "Golden Dawn term (Kalisch term)".}

Section Two

The twelve simple consonants HB:Heh, Vau, Zain, Chet, Tet, Yod, Lamed, Nun, Samekh, Ayin, Tzaddi & Qof symbolize also twelve oblique points {The Order of the Golden Dawn says, in order: North East, HB:Heh ; South East, HB:Vau ; East Above, HB:Zain ; East Below, HB:Chet ; North Above, HB:Tet ; North Below, HB:Yod ; North West, HB:Lamed ; South West, HB:Nun ; West Above, HB:Samekh ; West Below, HB:Ayin ; South Above, HB:Tzaddi ; and South Below, HB:Qof. The Kalish translation gives in the same order for the letters: East Height, North East, East Depth, South Height, South East, South Depth, West Height, South West, West Depth, North Height, North West, North Depth.}. They

ספר יצירה

grew wider and wider to all eternity, and these are the boundaries of the world. {In the Golden Dawn theory, as developed by Paul Foster Case, the posthumous founder of B.O.T.A., these 12 directions are the locations of the twelve edges of the "Cube of Space" which has for faces the first six double letters. Some Qabalistic studies attempt to define a diamond shape in three dimensions. In any event, this section is possibly the origin of the Masonic Temple of Solomon, which fills the universe through its duplication -- like three-dimensional tiles fitting together.}

Section Three

The twelve simple letters HB:Heh, Vau, Zain, Chet, Tet, Yod, Lamed, Nun, Samekh, Ayin, Tzaddi & Qof fundamentally, having been designed, established, combined, weighed and exchanged by Him, He performed by them: twelve constellations in the world, twelve months in the year, and twelve organs in the human body, male and female.

Section Four

The twelve constellations in the world are: Aries, Taurus, Gemini, Cancer, Leo, Virgo, Libra, Scorpio, Sagittarius Capricorn Aquarius and Pisces. The twelve {Hebrew} months of the year are: Nisan {the seventh month}, Ivar, Sivan, Tamus, Ab, Elul, Tishri, Mavcheshvan {also called Chesvan} Kislev, Tebet, Shebat and Adar. The twelve organs of the human body are: two hands two feet, two kidneys, gall, small intestines, liver, esophagus, stomach and milt (either the spleen or reproductive organs. Both systems have been often confused in Theosophical writings and ancient sources. The degree of absurdity involved in this relationship is incredible. This presumes a "rape" ethos in the culture, owing to the association of violence to the spleen and sex to the genitals.}

Section Five

First Division. God let the letter HB:Heh predominate in Sight {K.T. is Speech}, crowned it, combined one with the other and formed by them: Aries in the world, the month Nisan in the Year, and the right foot of the human body, male and female.

Section Six

Second Division. He let the letter HB:Vau predominate in Hearing {K.T. is Thinking}, crowned it combined one with the other, and formed by them: Taurus in the world, the month Iyar in the year and the right kidney of the human body, male and female.

Section Seven

Third Division. He let the letter HB:Zain predominate in Smell {K.T. is Walking}, crowned it, combined one with the other, and formed by them: Gemini in the world, the month Sivan in the year, and the left foot of the human body, male and female.

Section Eight

ספר יצירה

First Division. He let the letter HB:Chet predominate in Speech {K.T. gives Seeing}, crowned it, combined one with the other, and formed by them: Cancer in the world, the month Tamus in the year, and the right hand of the human body, male and female.

Section Nine

Second Division. He let the letter HB:Tet predominate in Digestion or Swallowing {K.T. gives Hearing}, crowned it, combined one with the other, and formed by them: Leo in the world, the month Ab in the year, and the left kidney of the human body, male and female.

Section Ten

Third Division. He let the letter HB:Yod predominate in Touch or Coition {K.T. gives Working}, crowned it, combined one with the other, and formed by them Virgo in the world, the month Elul in the year, and the left hand of the human body, male and female.

Section Eleven

First Division. He let the letter HB:Lamed predominate in Work {K.T. says Coition}, crowned it, combined one with the other, and formed by them: Libra in the world, the month Tishri in the year, and the gall of the human body, male and female.

Section Twelve

Second Division. He let the letter HB:Nun predominate in Motion or Walking {K.T. says Smelling}, crowned it, combined one with the other, and formed by them: Scorpio in the world, the month Marcheshvan in the year, and the small intestines of the human body, male and female.

Section Thirteen

Third Division. He let the letter HB:Samekh predominate in Anger {K.T. says Sleep}, crowned it, combined one with the other, and formed by them: Sagittarius in the world, the month Kislev in the year, and the stomach of the human body, male and female.

Section Fourteen

First Division. He let the letter HB:Ayin predominate in Laughter {K.T. assigns Anger}, crowned it, combined one with the other, and formed by them: Capricorn in the world, the month Tebes in the year, and the liver in the human body, male and female.

Section Fifteen

Second Division. He let the letter HB:Tzaddi predominate in Meditation or Thinking {K.T. assigns Swallowing}, crowned it, combined one with the other, and formed by them: Aquarius in the world, the month Schwat in the year, and the esophagus of the human body, male and female.

Section Six

ספר יצירה

Third Division, He let the letter HB:Qof predominate in Sleep {K.T. assigns Laughing}, crowned it, combined one with the other, and formed by them: Pisces in the world, the month Adar in the year, and the milt of the human body, male and female.

He made them as a conflict, drew them up like a wall; and set one against the other as in warfare.

{This last point is explained by the observation that these twelve letters symbolize processes in human behavior that can interfere with each other. Some further points must now be made regarding the assignments of qualities and body parts to these twelve simple letters. In the Golden Dawn Tradition, many things are subordinated to the Astrological symbolism. This was true in the case of the Double letters, where one of several natural methods of assignment in the "Yetzirah" was passed over to provide a better match between the Double Letters and the planets to work with Tarot Trumps. The other methods do not work as well with the G.'. D.'. Tarot-Astrological system, and they are therefore excluded from "Liber 777". This should not make the student think that the primary method used there excludes the several systems proposed here. It is best to begin with a simple system. The serious student then must examine the other systems to determine the information contained in each of them. In the case of these Twelve Simple Letters, this is even more the case. The Golden Dawn -- "Liber 777" system has shifted the twelve qualities of the simple letters to make them match the usual qualities of the Astrological signs. The "Yetzirah" has set up an entirely new parallel system through these qualities which deserves its own study. The same is true of the body organs mentioned here. In the Golden Dawn system, these associations are omitted entirely. The usual associations to the Zodiac signs are assumed in place of these associations in the "Yetzirah" to body organs. It is suggested that these associations have a particular meaning of their own, and that the serious student will in time find it useful to study that system. By all means, begin with the simpler approach given in "Liber 777" and in the various works derived from the Order of the Golden Dawn. When comfortable with that approach, consider these other systems. It is the work of the advanced student of the mysteries to make these apparently diverse systems function well together -- even if the war of the simple letters is the only manner in which it may be done.

Always remember that the ideas presented in the "Yetzirah" are like words in their effect. The object is to first learn the simple uses of these ideas, and then to discover the uses of these ideas that are like circumlocutions, figures of speech and allegories. By that means, one can obtain the conversation of the Angels.}

ספר יצירה

Sepher Yetzirah *Book of Creation*

Chapter Six

Section One

These are the three mothers or the first elements Aleph, Mem, and Shin, from which emanated three progenitors: primitive air, water and fire, and from which emanated as their offspring three progenitors and their offspring, namely: the seven planets and their hosts, and the twelve oblique points.

{The production of the double and single letters from the mother letters is like the interaction of the mother letters in the six rings: Example; Beth is like Aleph combined with Shin, HB:Gemel = HB:Aleph + HB:Mem, HB:Dalet = HB:Shin + HB:Mem, HB:Koph = HB:Bet + HB:Lamed, HB:Peh = HB:Bet + HB:Dalet, HB:Resh = HB:Dalet + HB:Gemel, HB:Taw = HB:Aleph + HB:Shin + HB:Mem = HB:Bet + HB:Gemel + HB:Dalet = HB:Koph + HB:Peh + HB:Resh, HB:Heh = HB:Aleph + HB:Koph, HB:Vau = HB:Aleph + HB:Peh, HB:Zain = HB:Aleph + HB:Resh, HB:Chet = HB:Aleph + HB:Taw, HB:Tet = HB:Shin + HB:Koph, HB:Yod = HB:Shin + HB:Peh, HB:Lamed = HB:Shin + HB:Resh, HB:Nun + HB:Shin + HB:Taw, HB:Samekh = HB:Mem + HB:Koph, HB:Ayin = HB:Mem + HB:Peh, HB:Tzaddi = HB:Mem + HB:Resh, HB:Qof = HB:Mem + HB:Taw -- this is obtained from the symbolic meaning of the letters and the dictionary meanings of the words they can be made to form. It is not simply related to the sounds of the letters or to their number values, although a complex relationship does exist through gematria. This theoretical example

ספר יצירה

of the interrelationship of the letters is taken with permission from "Brief Meanings of the Hebrew Letters" by Bill Heidrick, copyright 1974 e.v.}

Section Two

To confirm this there are faithful witnesses; the world, year and man, the twelve, the Equipoise {Fire, Water and Air in balance}, the heptade {seven-fold nature of things}, which He regulates like the Dragon {Tali or the constellation Draco with its head and tail now taken in the simplified modern Astrology as the nodes of the Moon} sphere {the Hebrew word here is Galgal. It has the meaning of "machinery like turning wheels which drives the universe} and the heart {besides all this argument, it feels right}.

Section Three

The first elements Aleph, Mem and Shin are air, water and fire; the fire is above, the water below, and a breath of air establishes the balance among them. For an illustration may serve, that the fire carries the water, is the phonetic character of HB:Mem which is mute and HB:Shin is hissing like fire, there is HB:Aleph among them, a breath of air which places them in equilibrium.

Section Four

Dragon {Tali} is in the world like a king upon his throne, the sphere is in the year like a king in the empire, and the heart is in the human body like a king in war. {Thus the three mother letters are like Draco, the seven double letters are like the regular motions of the planets and the twelve single letters are like the easily upset functions of the body.}

Section Five

Elohim has also set the one over against the other; the good against the evil, and the evil against the good {here "good" is the Hebrew word "tob" which is the seal of creation used in Genesis and "evil" is "Ra" the name used by the Egyptians for the god of the sun -- a competitor of Jehovah}; the good proceeds from the good, and the evil from the evil; the good purifies the bad, and the bad the good; the good is preserved for the good, and the evil for the bad ones {The Qabalistic ideas of good and evil are very different from those of modern society. Avoid a moral interpretation here. In simple terms, "good" = "our side" and "evil" = "anything against us." The Qabalistic ideas are more complex than that, and they involve concepts much like those met in law courts.}.

Section Six

There are three of which every one of them stands by itself; one is in the affirmative, the other in the negative and one equalizes them {The three mother letters are viewed as plaintiff, defendant and judge}.

Section Seven

ספר יצירה

There are seven of which three are against three and one places them in equilibrium. There are twelve which are all the time at war; three of them produce love, and three hatred, three are animators and three destroyers {Beth vs. Gimel, Dalet vs. Koph, Peh vs. Resh with Taw placing them in equilibrium. As for the twelve which are at war, that matter depends on association to body parts and directions -- it is not clearly defined in the "Sepher Yetzirah", but needs more study.}.

Section Eight

The three that produce love are the heart and the ears; the three that produce hatred are the liver, the gall and the tongue; the three animators are the two nostrils and the milt; and the three destroyers are the mouth and the two openings of the body; and God, the faithful King rules over all from His holy habitation to all eternity. He is one above three, three are above seven, seven are above twelve, and all are linked together. {If the text is not corrupt in Section Eight, we may understand that: Gimel, Peh and either Aleph, Taw or Vau produce love; Lamed, Ayin and perhaps Taw produce hatred; Dalet, Resh and Qof are the animators; Peh and two other Letters are the destroyers. The issue is not clear.}

Section Nine

There are twenty-two letters by which the I AM {HB:Aleph-Nun-Yod-Heh}, Yah {HB:Yod-Heh}, He of the Hosts {HB:Yod-Heh-Vau-Heh Tzaddi-Bet-Aleph-Vau-Taw}, God Almighty {HB:Aleph-Lamed Shin-Dalet-Yod}, He Who Creates the Eiohim

Sepher Yetzirah   Book of Creation

{HB:Yod -Heh-Vau-Heh Aleph-Lamed-Heh-Yod-Memfinal}, designed, formed and created by three Sepharim, His whole world, and formed by them creatures and all those that will be formed in time to come.

Section Ten

When the Patriarch Abraham comprehended the great truism, revolved it in his mind, conceived it perfectly, made careful investigations and profound inquiries, pondered upon it and succeeded in contemplations, the Lord of the Universe appeared to him, called him his friend, made with him a covenant between the ten fingers of his hands, which is the covenant of the tongue, and the covenant between the ten toes of his feet, which is the covenant of circumcision, and said of him: "Before I formed thee in the belly I knew thee." {Jer.1.5}

THUS ENDS

HB:Samekh-Peh-Resh Yod-Tzaddi-Yod-Resh-Heh

ספר יצירה

Sepher Yetzirah   Book of Creation

Sepher Yetzirah
Westcott Translation

Translated from the Hebrew by

Wm. Wynn Westcott

1887

ספר יצירה

Sepher Yetzirah   *Book of Creation*

PREFACE NOTE

(NOTE: The *Sepher Yetzirah* is one of the most famous of the ancient Qabalistic texts. It was first put into writing around 200 C.E. Westcott's Translation of the Sepher Yetzirah was a primary source for the rituals and Knowledge Lectures of the Golden Dawn. This is the Third Edition of Westcott's translation, first published in 1887.)

INTRODUCTION

The "Sepher Yetzirah," or "Book of Formation," is perhaps the oldest Rabbinical treatise of Kabalistic philosophy which is still extant. The great interest which has been evinced of late years in the Hebrew Kabalah, and the modes of thought and doctrine allied to it, has induced me to translate this tractate from the original Hebrew texts, and to collate with them the Latin versions of mediaeval authorities; and I have also published *An Introduction to the Kabalah* which may be found useful to students.

Three important books of the "Zohar," or "Book of Splendour," which is a great storehouse of Kabalistic teaching, have been translated into English by S. L. MacGregor Mathers, and the "Sepher Yetzirah" in an English translation is almost a necessary

ספר יצירה

companion to these abstruse disquisitions: the two books indeed mutually explain each other.

The "Sepher Yetzirah," although this name means "The Book of Formation," is not in any sense a narrative of Creation, or a substitute Genesis, but is an ancient and instructive philosophical treatise upon one aspect of the origin of the universe and mankind; an aspect at once archaic and essentially Hebrew. The grouping of the processes of origin into an arrangement, at once alphabetic and numeral, is one only to be found in Semitic authors.

Attention must be called to the essential peculiarity of the Hebrew language, the inextricable and necessary association of numbers and letters; every letter suggesting a number, and every group of letters having a numerical signification, as vital as its literal meaning.

The Kabalistic principles involved in the reversal of Hebrew letters, and their substitution by others, on definite schemes, should also be studied and borne in mind.

It is exactly on these principles that the "ground-work idea" 'of this disquisition rests; and these principles may be traced throughout the Kabalistic tractates which have succeeded it in point of time and development, many of which are associated together in one volume known as the "Zohar," which is in the main concerned with the essential dignities of the Godhead, with the Emanations which have sprung therefrom, with the doctrine of the Sephiroth, the ideals of

Sepher Yetzirah   Book of Creation

Macroprosopus and Microprosopus, and the doctrine of Reincarnation.

The "Sepher Yetzirah," on the other hand, is mainly concerned with our universe and with the Microcosm. The opinions of Hebrew Kabalistic Rabbis and of modern mystics may be fitly introduced here.

The following interesting quotation is from Rabbi Moses Botarel, who wrote his famous Commentary in 1409:--"It was Abraham our Father--blessed be he--who wrote this book to condemn the doctrine of the sages of his time, who were incredulous of the supreme dogma of the Unity. At least, this was the opinion of Rabbi Saadiah--blessed be he--as written in the first chapter of his book *The Philosopher's Stone.* These are his words: The sages of Babylon attacked Abraham on account of his faith; for they were all against him although themselves separable into three sects. The First thought that the Universe was subject to the control of two opposing forces, the one existing but to destroy the other, this is dualism; they held that there was nothing in common between the author of evil and the author of good. The Second sect admitted Three great Powers; two of them as in the first case, and a third Power whose function was to decide between the two others, a supreme arbitrator. The Third sect recognised no god beside the Sun, in which it recognised the sole principle of existence."

Rabbi Judah Ha Lévi (who flourished about 1120), in his critical description of this treatise, wrote: "The Sepher Yetzirah teaches us the existence of a Single Divine Power by shewing us that in the

ספר יצירה

bosom of variety and multiplicity there is a Unity and Harmony, and that such universal concord could only arise from the rule of a Supreme Unity."

According to Isaac Myer, in his *Quabbalah* (p. 159), the "Sepher Yetzirah" was referred to in the writings of Ibn Gebirol of Cordova, commonly called Avicebron, who died in A.D. 1070.

Eliphas Levi, the famous French Occultist, thus wrote of the "Sepher Yetzirah," in his *Histoire de la Magie*, p. 54: "The Zohar is a Genesis of illumination, the Sepher Jezirah is a ladder formed of truths. Therein are explained the thirty-two absolute signs of sounds, numbers and letters: each letter reproduces a number, an idea and a form; so that mathematics are capable of application to ideas and to forms not less rigorously than to numbers, by exact proportion and perfect correspondence. By the science of the Sepher Jezirah the human spirit is fixed to truth, and in reason, and is able to take account of the possible development of intelligence by the evolutions of numbers. The Zohar represents absolute truth, and the Sepher Jezirah provides the means by which we may seize, appropriate and make use of it."

Upon another page Eliphas Lévi writes: "The Sepher Jezirah and the Apocalypse are the masterpieces of Occultism; they contain more wisdom than words; their expression is as figurative as poetry, and at the same time it is as exact as mathematics.

Sepher Yetzirah   Book of Creation

In the volume entitled *La Kabbale* by the eminent French scholar, Adolphe Franck, there is a chapter on the "Sepher Yetzirah." He writes as follows:--

"The Book of Formation contains, I will not say system of physics, but of cosmology such as could be conceived at an age and in a country where the habit of explaining all phenomena by the immediate action of the First Cause, tended to check the spirit of observation, and where in consequence certain general and superficial relations perceived in the natural world passed for the science of Nature."..."Its form is simple and grave; there is nothing like a demonstration nor an argument; but it consists rather of a series of aphorisms, regularly grouped, and which have all the conciseness of the most ancient oracles."

In his analysis of the "Sepher Yetzirah," he adds:--"The Book of Formation, even if it be not very voluminous, and if it do not altogether raise us to very elevated regions of thought, yet offers us at least a composition which is very homogeneous and of a rare originality. The clouds which the imagination of commentators have gathered around it, will be dissipated, if we look for, in it, not mysteries of ineffable wisdom, but an attempt at a reasonable doctrine, made when reason arose, an effort to grasp the plan of the universe, and to secure the link which binds to one common principle, all the elements which are around us."

"The last word of this system is the substitution of the absolute divine Unity for every idea of Dualism, for that pagan philosophy which saw in matter an eternal substance whose laws were not in

ספר יצירה

accord with Divine Will; and for the Biblical doctrine, which by its idea of Creation, postulates two things, the Universe and God, as two substances absolutely distinct one from the other.

"In fact, in the 'Sepher Yetzirah,' God considered as the Infinite and consequently the indefinable Being, extended throughout all things by his power and existence, is while above, yet not outside of numbers, sounds and letters--the principles and general laws which we recognise."

"Every element has its source from a higher form, and all things have their common origin from the Word (*Logos*), the Holy Spirit…. So God is at once, in the highest sense, both the matter and the form of the universe. Yet He is not *only* that form; for nothing can or does exist outside of Himself; His substance is the foundation of all, and all things bear His imprint and are symbols of His intelligence."

Hebrew tradition assigns the doctrines of the oldest portions of the "Zohar" to a date antecedent to the building of the Second Temple, but Rabbi Simeon ben Jochai, who lived in the reign of the Emperor Titus, A.D. 70-80, is considered to have been the first to commit these to writing, and Rabbi Moses de Leon, of Guadalaxara, in Spain, who died in 1305, certainly reproduced and published the "Zohar."

Ginsburg, speaking of the Zoharic doctrines of the Ain Suph, says that they were unknown until the thirteenth century, but he does not deny the great antiquity of the "Sepher Yetzirah," in which it will be noticed the "Ain Suph Aur" and "Ain Suph" are not mentioned. I suggest, however, that this omission is no proof that the doctrines of "Ain Suph Aur" and "Ain Suph" did not then exist, because it is a reasonable supposition that the "Sepher Yetzirah" was the volume assigned to the Yetziratic World, the third of the four Kabalistic Worlds of Emanation, while the "Asch Metzareph" is concerned with the Assiatic, fourth, or lowest World of Shells, and is on the face of it an alchemical treatise; and again the "Siphra Dtzenioutha" may be fittingly considered to be an Aziluthic work, treating of the Emanations of Deity alone; and there was doubtless a fourth work assigned to the World of Briah--the second type, but I have not been able to identify this treatise. Both the Babylonian and the Jerusalem Talmuds refer to the "Sepher Yetzirah." Their treatise, named "Sanhedrin," certainly mentions the "Book of Formation," and another similar work; and Rashi in his commentary on the treatise "Erubin," considers this a reliable historical notice. Other historical notices are those of Saadya Gaon, who died A.D. 940, and Judah Ha Levi, A.D. 1150; both these Hebrew classics speak of it as a very ancient work. Some modern critics have attributed the authorship to the Rabbi Akiba, who lived in the time of the Emperor Hadrian, A.D. 120, and lost his life in supporting the claims of Barchocheba, a false messiah: others suggest it was first written about A.D. 200.

Graetz however assigns it to early Gnostic times, third or fourth century, and Zunz speaks of it as post Talmudical, and belonging to the Geonim period 700-800 A.D.; Rubinsohn, in the *Bibliotheca Sacra*, speaks of this latter idea as having no real basis.

ספר יצירה

The Talmuds were first collected into a concrete whole, and printed in Venice, 1520 A.D.

The "Zohar" was first printed in Mantua in 1558; again in Cremona, 1560; and at Lublin, 1623; and a fourth edition by Knorr von Rosenroth, at Sulzbach in 1684. Some parts are not very ancient, because the Crusades are mentioned in one chapter. Six extant Hebrew editions of the "Sepher Yetzirah" were collected and printed at Lemberg in 1680. The oldest of these six recensions was that of Saadjah Gaon (by some critics called spurious). There are still extant three Latin versions, *viz.*, that of Gulielmus Postellus; one by Johann Pistorius; and a third by Joannes Stephanus Rittangelius; this latter gives both Hebrew and Latin versions, and also "The Thirty-Two Paths" as a supplement.

There is a German translation, by Johann Friedrich von Meyer, dated 1830; a version by Isidor Kalisch, in which he has reproduced many of the valuable annotations of Meyer; an edition in French by Papus, 1888; an edition in French by Mayer Lambert, 1891, with the Arabic Commentary of Saadya Gaon; and an English edition by Peter Davidson, 1896, to which are added "The Fifty Gates of Intelligence" and "The Thirty-Two Ways of Wisdom." The edition which I now offer is fundamentally that of the ancient Hebrew codices translated into English, and collated with the Latin versions of Pistorius, Postellus, and Rittangelius, following the latter, rather than the former commentators. As to the authenticity of "The Sepher Yetzirah," students may refer to the *Bibliotheca magna Rabbinica* of Bartoloccio de Cellerio, Rome, 1678-1692; to Basnage, *History of the Jews*, 1708; and to *The Doctrine and*

Sepher Yetzirah   *Book of Creation*

Literature of the Kabalah, by A. B. Waite, 1902. The following copies of the "Sepher Yetzirah" in Hebrew, I have also examined, but only in a superficial manner:--

1. A Version by Saadiah, Ab. ben David, and three others, Mantua, 1562, 4to.

2. A Version with the commentary of Rabbi Abraham F. Dior, Amsterdam, 1642, 4to.

3. A Version with preface by M. ben J. Chagiz, Amsterdam, 1713, 16mo. 4. A Version, Constantinople, 1719, 8vo.

5. " " Zolkiew, 1745, 4to.

6. " " by Moses ben Jacob, Zozec, 1779, 4to.

7. " " Grodno, 1806, 4to.

8. " " Dyhernfurth, 1812, 8vo.

9. " " Salonica, 1831, 8vo.

10. A MS. copy dated 1719, in the British Museum.

I add here the full titles of the three Latin versions; they are all to be found in the British Museum Library.

"Abrahami Patriarchae Liber Jezirah sive Formationis Mundi, Patribus quidem Abrahami tempora praecedentibus revelatus, sed

ספר יצירה

ab ipso etiam Abrahamo expositus Isaaco, et per pro prophetarum manus posteritati conservatus, ipsis autem 72 Mosis auditoribus in secundo divinae veritatis loco, hoc est in ratione, quoe est posterior authoritate, habitus." Parisiis, 1552. Gulielmus Postellus."Id est Liber Jezirah, qui Abrahamo, Patriarchae adscribitur, una cum Commentario Rabbi Abraham F.D. super 32 semitis Sapientiae, a quibus Liber Jezirah incipit: Translatus et notis illustratus a Joanne Stephano Rittangelio, Ling. Orient. in Elect. Acad. Regiomontana Prof. Extraord," Amstelodami, 1642.In Tomas Primus of "Artis Cabalisticae hoc est reconditae theologiae et philosophiae scriptorum." Basileae 1587, is found "Liber de Creatione Cabalistinis, Hebraice Sepher Jezira; Authore Abrahamo. Successive filiis ore traditus. Hinc jam rebus Israel inclinatis ne deficeret per sapientes Hierusalem arcanis et profundissimis sensibus literis commendatus." Johannes Pistorius.

The "Sepher Yetzirah" consists of six chapters, having 33 paragraphs distributed among them, in this manner: the first has 12, then follow 5, 5, 4, 3, and 4.

Yet in some versions the paragraphs and subject-matter are found in a different arrangement. The oldest title has, as an addition, the words, "The Letters of our Father Abraham" or "ascribed to the patriarch Abraham," and it is spoken of as such by many mediaeval authorities: but this origin is doubtless fabulous, although perhaps not more improbable than the supposed authorship of the "Book of Enoch," mentioned by St. Jude, of which two MSS. copies in the Ethiopic language were rescued from the wilds of Abyssinia in 1773 by the great traveller James Bruce. In essence this work was, doubtless, the crystallisation of centuries of tradition, by one writer, and it has been added to from time to time, by later authors, who have also revised it. Some of the additions, which were rejected even by mediaeval students, I have not incorporated with the text at all, and I present in this volume only the undoubted kernel of this occult nut, upon which many great authorities, Hebrew, German, Jesuit and others, have written long Commentaries, and yet have failed to explain satisfactorily. I find Kalisch, speaking of these Commentaries, says, "they contain nothing but a medley of arbitrary explanations, and sophistical distortions of scriptural verses, astrological notions, Oriental superstitions, a metaphysical jargon, a poor knowledge of physics, and not a correct elucidation of this ancient book." Kalisch, however, was not an occultist; these commentaries are, however, so extensive as to demand years of study, and I feel no hesitation in confessing that my researches into them have been but superficial. For convenience of study I have placed the Notes in a separate form at the end of the work, and I have made a short definition of the subject-matter of each chapter. The substance of this little volume was read as Lecture before "The Hermetic Society of London," in the summer of 1886, Dr. Anna Kingsford, President, in the chair. Some of the Notes were the explanations given verbally, and subsequently in writing, to members of the Society who asked for information upon abstruse points in the "Sepher," and for collateral doctrines; others, of later date, are answers which have been given to students of Theosophy and Hermetic philosophy, and to my pupils of the Study Groups of the Rosicrucian Society of England.

ספר יצירה

Sepher Yetzirah   *Book of Creation*

CHAPTER I

Section 1. In thirty-two ⁽¹⁾ mysterious Paths of Wisdom did Jah, ⁽²⁾ the Jehovah of hosts, ⁽³⁾ the God of Israel, ⁽⁴⁾ the Living Elohim, ⁽⁵⁾ the King of ages, the merciful and gracious God, ⁽⁶⁾ the Exalted One, the Dweller in eternity, most high and holy--engrave his name by the three Sepharim ⁽⁷⁾) --Numbers, Letters, and Sounds.⁽⁸⁾

2. Ten are the ineffable Sephiroth. ⁽⁹⁾ Twenty-two are the Letters, the Foundation of all things; there are Three Mothers, Seven Double and Twelve ⁽¹⁰⁾ Simple letters.

3. The ineffable Sephiroth are Ten, as are the Numbers; and as there are in man five fingers over against five, so over them is established a covenant of strength, by word of mouth, and by the circumcision of the flesh. ⁽¹¹⁾

4. Ten is the number of the ineffable Sephiroth, ten and not nine, ten and not eleven. Understand this wisdom, and be wise by the perception. Search out concerning it, restore the Word to its creator, and replace Him who formed it upon his throne. ⁽¹²⁾ .

5. The Ten ineffable Sephiroth have ten vast regions bound unto them; boundless in origin and having no ending; an abyss ⁽¹³⁾ of good and of ill; measureless height and depth; boundless to the East and the West; boundless to the North and South; ⁽¹⁴⁾ and the Lord

ספר יצירה

the only God, [15] the Faithful King rules all these from his holy seat, [16] for ever and ever.

6. The Ten ineffable Sephiroth have the appearance of the Lightning flash, [17] their origin is unseen and no end is perceived. The Word is in them as they rush forth and as they return, they speak as from the whirl-wind, and returning fall prostrate in adoration before the Throne.

7. The Ten ineffable Sephiroth, whose ending is even as their origin, are like as a flame arising from a burning coal. For God [18] is superlative in his Unity, there is none equal unto Him: what number canst thou place before One.

8. Ten are the ineffable Sephiroth; seal up thy lips lest thou speak of them, and guard thy heart as thou considerest them; and if thy mind escape from thee bring it back to thy control; even as it was said, "running and returning" (the living creatures ran and returned) [19] and hence was the Covenant made.

9. The ineffable Sephiroth give forth the Ten numbers. First; the Spirit of the God of the living; [20] Blessed and more than blessed be the Living God [21] of ages. The Voice, the Spirit, and the Word, [22] these are the Holy Spirit.

10. Second; from the Spirit He produced Air, and formed in it twenty-two sounds--the letters; three are mothers, seven are double, and twelve are simple; but the Spirit is first and above these. Third; from the Air He formed the Waters, and from the formless and void

Sepher Yetzirah   Book of Creation

(23) made mire and clay, and designed surfaces upon them, and hewed recesses in them, and formed the strong material foundation. Fourth; from the Water He formed Fire (24) and made for Himself a Throne of Glory with Auphanim, Seraphim and Kerubim, (25) as his ministering angels; and with these three (26) he completed his dwelling, as it is written, "Who maketh his angels spirits and his ministers a flaming fire." (27)

11. He selected three letters from among the simple ones and sealed them and formed them into a Great Name, I H V, (28) and with this He sealed the universe in six directions.

Fifth; He looked above, and sealed the Height with I H V.

Sixth; He looked below, and sealed the Depth with I V H.

Seventh; He looked forward, and sealed the East with H I V.

Eighth; He looked backward, and sealed the West with H V I.

Ninth; He looked to the right, and sealed the South with V I H.

Tenth; He looked to the left, and sealed the North with V H I.

12. Behold! From the Ten ineffable Sephiroth do, proceed--the One Spirit of the Gods of the living, Air, Water, Fire; and also Height, Depth, East, West, South and North. (29)

ספר יצירה

CHAPTER II

Section 1. The twenty-two sounds and letters are the Foundation of all things. Three mothers, seven doubles and twelve simples. The Three Mothers are Aleph, Mem and Shin, they are Air, Water and Fire Water is silent, Fire is sibilant, and Air derived from the Spirit is as the tongue of a balance standing between these contraries which are in equilibrium, reconciling and mediating between them.

2. He hath formed, weighed, and composed with these twenty-two letters every created thing, and the form of everything which shall hereafter be.

3. These twenty-two sounds or letters are formed by the voice, impressed on the air, and audibly modified in five places; in the throat, in the mouth, by the tongue, through the teeth, and by the lips. [31]

4. These twenty-two letters, which are the foundation of all things, He arranged as upon a sphere with two hundred and thirty-one gates, and the sphere may be rotated forward or backward, whether for good or for evil; from the good comes true pleasure, from evil nought but torment.

5. For He shewed the combination of these letters, each with the other; Aleph with all, and all with Aleph; Beth with all, and all with

ספר יצירה

Beth. Thus in combining all together in pairs are produced the two hundred and thirty-one gates of knowledge. ⁽³²⁾

6. And from the non-existent ⁽³³⁾ He made Something; and all forms of speech and everything that has been produced; from the empty void He made the material world, and from the inert earth He brought forth everything that hath life. He hewed, as it were, vast columns out of the intangible air, and by the power of His Name made every creature and everything that is; and the production of all things from the twenty-two letters is the proof that they are all but parts of one living body. ⁽³⁴⁾

Sepher Yetzirah *Book of Creation*

a m c

CHAPTER III

Section 1. The Foundation of all the other sounds and letters is provided by the Three Mothers, Aleph, Mem and Shin; they resemble a Balance, on the one hand the guilty, on the other hand the purified, and Aleph the Air is like the Tongue of a Balance standing between them. [35]

2. The Three Mothers, Aleph, Mem and Shin, are a great Mystery, very admirable and most recondite, and sealed as with six rings; and from them proceed Air, Fire, and Water, which divide into active and passive forces. The Three Mothers, Aleph, Mem and Shin, are the Foundation, from them spring three Fathers, and from these have proceeded all things that are in the world.

3. The Three Mothers in the world are Aleph, Mem and Shin: the heavens [36] were produced [37] from Fire; the earth from the Water; and the Air from the Spirit is as a reconciler between the Fire and the Water.

4. The Three Mothers, Aleph, Mem and Shin, Fire, Water and Air, are shown in the Year: from the fire came heat, from the waters came cold, and from the air was produced the temperate state, again a mediator between them. The Three Mothers, Aleph, Mem and Shin, Fire, Water and Air, are found in Man: from the fire was

ספר יצירה

formed the head; from the water the belly; and from the air was formed the chest, again placed as a mediator between the others.

5. These Three Mothers did He produce and design, and combined them; and He sealed them as the three mothers in the Universe, in the Year and in Man--both male and female. He caused the letter Aleph to reign in Air and crowned it, and combining it with the others He sealed it, as Air in the World, as the temperate (climate) of the Year, and as the breath in the chest (the lungs for breathing air) in Man: the male with Aleph, Mem, Shin, the female with Shin, Mem, Aleph. He caused the letter Mem to reign in Water, crowned it, and combining it with the others formed the earth in the world, cold in the year, and the belly in man, male and female, the former with Mem, Aleph, Shin, the latter with Mem, Shin, Aleph. He caused Shin to reign in Fire, and crowned it, and combining it with the others sealed with it the heavens in the universe, heat in the year and the head in man, male and female. [38]

Sepher Yetzirah   *Book of Creation*

ת ר פ כ ד ג ב

CHAPTER IV

Section 1. The Seven double letters, Beth, Gimel, Daleth, Kaph, Peh, Resh, and Tau have each two sounds associated with them. They are referred to Life, Peace, Wisdom, Riches, Grace, Fertility and Power. The two sounds of each letter are the hard and the soft-- the aspirated and the softened. They are called Double, because each letter presents a contrast or permutation; thus Life and Death; Peace and War; Wisdom and Folly; Riches and Poverty; Grace and Indignation; Fertility and Solitude; Power and Servitude.

2. These Seven Double Letters point out seven localities; Above, Below, East, West, North, South, and the Palace of Holiness in the midst of them sustaining all things.

3. These Seven Double Letters He designed, produced, and combined, and formed with them the Planets of this World, the Days of the Week, and the Gates of the soul (the orifices of perception) in Man. From these Seven He bath produced the Seven Heavens, the Seven Earths, the Seven Sabbaths: for this cause He has loved and blessed the number Seven more than all things under Heaven (His Throne).

ספר יצירה

4. Two Letters produce two houses; three form six; four form twenty-four; five form one hundred and twenty; six form seven hundred and twenty; [39] seven form five thousand and forty; and beyond this their numbers increase so that the mouth can hardly utter them, nor the ear hear the number of them. So now, behold the Stars of our World, the Planets which are Seven; the Sun, Venus, Mercury, Moon, Saturn, Jupiter and Mars. The Seven are also the Seven Days of Creation; and the Seven Gateways of the Soul of Man--the two eyes, the two ears, the mouth and the two nostrils. So with the Seven are formed the seven heavens, [41] the seven earths, and the seven periods of time; and so has He preferred the number Seven above all things under His Heaven. [42]

Supplement to Chapter IV

NOTE.--This is one of several modern illustrations of the allotment of the Seven Letters; it is not found in the ancient copies of the "Sepher Yetzirah."

He produced Beth, and referred it to Wisdom ; He crowned it, combined and formed with it the Moon in the Universe, the first day of the week, and the right eye of man.

He produced Gimel, and referred it to Health; He crowned it, combined and joined with it Mars in the Universe, the second day of the week, and the right ear of man.

Sepher Yetzirah   *Book of Creation*

He produced Daleth, and referred it to Fertility; He crowned it, combined and formed with it the Sun in the Universe, the third day of the week, and the right nostril of man.

He produced Kaph, and referred it to Life; He crowned it, combined and formed with it Venus in the Universe, the fourth day of the week, and the left eye of man.

He produced Peh, and referred it to Power; He crowned it, combined and formed with it Mercury in the Universe, the fifth day of the week, and the left ear of man.

He produced Resh, and referred it to Peace; He crowned it, combined and formed with it Saturn in the Universe, the sixth day of the week, and the left nostril of man.

He produced Tau, and referred it to Beauty; He crowned it, combined and formed with it Jupiter in the Universe, the Seventh Day of the week, and the mouth of man.

By these Seven letters were also made seven worlds, seven heavens, seven earths, seven seas, seven rivers, seven deserts, seven days, seven weeks from Passover to Pentecost, and every seventh year a Jubilee.

Mayer Lambert gives:--Beth to Saturn and the Hebrew Sabbath--that is Saturday; Gimel to Jupiter and Sunday; Daleth to Mars and Monday; Kaph to the Sun and Tuesday; Peh to Venus and

ספר יצירה

Wednesday; Resh to Mercury and Thursday; and Tau to the Moon and Friday.

Sepher Yetzirah   *Book of Creation*

h w z j   f y l n s u x q

CHAPTER V

1. The Twelve Simple Letters are Héh, Vau, Zain, Cheth, Teth, Yod, Lamed, Nun, Samech, Oin, Tzaddi and Qoph; [43] they are the foundations of these twelve properties: Sight, Hearing, Smell, Speech, Taste, Sexual Love, Work, Movement, Anger, Mirth, Imagination, [44] and Sleep. These Twelve are also allotted to the directions in space: North-east, South-east, the East above, the East below, the North above, the North below, the South-west, the Northwest, the West above, the West below, the South above, and the South below; these diverge to infinity, and are as the arms of the Universe.

2. These Twelve Simple Letters He designed, and combined, and formed with them the Twelve celestial constellations of the Zodiac, whose signs are Teth, Shin, Tau, Samech, Aleph, Beth, Mem, Oin, Qoph, Gimel, Daleth, and Daleth. [45] The Twelve are also the Months of the Year: Nisan, [46] Yiar, Sivan, Tamuz, Ab, Elul, Tishri, Hesvan, Kislev, Tebet, Sabat and Adar. The Twelve are also the Twelve organs of living creatures: [47] the two hands, the two feet, the two kidneys, the spleen, the liver, the gall, private parts, stomach and intestines.

He made these, as it were provinces, and arranged them as in order of battle for warfare. And also the Elohim [48] made one from the region of the other.

ספר יצירה

Three Mothers and Three Fathers; and thence issue Fire, Air and Water. Three Mothers, Seven Doubles and Twelve Simple letters and sounds.

3. Behold now these are the Twenty and Two Letters from which Jah, Jehovah Tzabaoth, the Living Elohim, the God of Israel, exalted and sublime, the Dweller in eternity, formed and established all things; High and Holy is His Name.

Supplement to Chapter V

NOTE.--This is a modern illustration of the allotment of the Twelve Letters; it is not found in the ancient copies of the "Sepher Yetzirah."

1. God produced Hé predominant in Speech, crowned it, combined and formed with it Aries in the Universe, Nisan in the Year, and the right foot of Man.

2. He produced Vau, predominant in mind, crowned it, combined and formed with it Taurus in the Universe, Aiar in the Year, and the right kidney of Man.

3. He produced Zain, predominant in Movement crowned it, combined and formed it with Gemini in the Universe, Sivan in the Year, and the left foot of Man.

4. He produced Cheth, predominant in Sight, crowned it, combined and formed it with Cancer in the Universe, Tammuz in the year, and the right hand of Man.

Sepher Yetzirah — Book of Creation

5. He produced Teth, predominant in Hearing, crowned it, combined and formed with it Leo in the Universe, Ab in the Year, and the left kidney in Man.

6. He produced Yod, predominant in Work, crowned it, combined and formed with it Virgo in the Universe, Elul in the Year, and the left hand of Man.

7. He produced Lamed, predominant in Sexual desire, crowned it, combined and formed with it Libra in the Universe, Tishri in the Year, and the private parts of Man. (Kalisch gives "gall.")

8. He produced Nun, predominant in Smell, crowned it, combined and formed with it Scorpio in the Universe, Heshvan in the Year, and the intestines of Man.

9. He produced Samech, predominant in Sleep, crowned it, combined and formed with it Sagittarius in the Universe, Kislev in the Year, and the stomach of Man.

10. He produced Oin, predominant in Anger, crowned it, combined and formed with it Capricornus in the Universe, Tebet in the Year, and the liver of Man.

11. He produced Tzaddi, predominant in Taste, crowned it, combined and formed with it Aquarius in the Year, and the gullet in Man).

ספר יצירה

12. He produced Qoph, predominant in Mirth, crowned it, combined and formed with it Pisces in the Universe, Adar in the Year, and the spleen of Man.

NOTE.--Mediaeval authorities and modern editors give very different allocations to the twelve simple letters.

CHAPTER VI

Section 1. Three Fathers and their generations, Seven conquerors and their armies, and Twelve bounds of the Universe. See now, of these words, the faithful witnesses are the Universe, the Year and Man. The dodecad, the heptad, and the triad with their provinces; above is the Celestial Dragon, T L I, [49] and below is the World, and lastly the heart of Man. The Three are Water, Air and Fire; Fire above, Water below, and Air conciliating between them; and the sign of these things is that the Fire sustains (volatilises) the waters; Mem is mute, Shin is sibilant, and Aleph is the Mediator and as it were a friend placed between them.

2. The Celestial Dragon, T L I, is placed over the universe like a king upon the throne; the revolution of the year is as a king over his dominion; the heart of man is as a king in warfare. Moreover, He made all things one from the other; and the Elohim set good over against evil, and made good things from good, and evil things from evil: with the good tested He the evil, and with the evil did He try the good. Happiness [50] is reserved for the good, and misery [51] is kept for the wicked.

3. The Three are One, and that One stands above. The Seven are divided; three are over against three, and one stands between the triads. The Twelve stand as in warfare; three are friends, three are enemies; three are life givers; three are destroyers. The three friends are the heart, the ears, and the mouth; the three enemies are the

ספר יצירה

liver, the gall, and the tongue; (52) while God (53) the faithful king rules over all. One above Three, Three above Seven, and Seven above Twelve: and all are connected the one with the other.

4. And after that our father Abraham had perceived and understood, and had taken down and engraved all these things, the Lord most high (55) revealed Himself, and called him His beloved, and made a Covenant with him and his seed; and Abraham believed on Him (56) and it was imputed unto him for righteousness. And He made this Covenant as between the ten toes of the feet--this is that of circumcision; and as between the ten fingers of the hands and this is that of the tongue. (57) And He formed the twenty-two letters into speech (58) and shewed him all the mysteries of them. (59) He drew them through the Waters; He burned them in the Fire; He vibrated them in the Air; Seven planets in the heavens, and Twelve celestial constellations of the stars of the Zodiac.

The End of "The Book of Formation

Sepher Yetzirah *Book of Creation*

THE FIFTY GATES OF INTELLIGENCE

Attached to some editions of the "Sepher Yetzirah" is found this scheme of Kabalistic classification of knowledge emanating from the Second Sephira Binah, Understanding, and descending by stages through the angels, heavens, humanity, animal and vegetable and mineral kingdoms to Hyle and the chaos. The Kabalists said that one must enter and pass up through the Gates to attain to the Thirty-two Paths of Wisdom; and that even Moses only passed through the forty-ninth Gate, and never entered the fiftieth. See the *Oedipus Aegyptiacus* of Athanasius Kircher, vol. ii. p. 319.

First Order: Elementary.

1. Chaos, Hyle, The first matter.
2. Formless, void, lifeless.
3. The Abyss.
4. Origin of the Elements.
5. Earth (no seed germs).
6. Water.
7. Air.
8. Fire
9. Differentiation of qualities.
10. Mixture and combination.

ספר יצירה

Second Order: Decad of Evolution.

11. Minerals differentiate.
12. Vegetable principles appear.
13. Seeds germinate in moisture.
14. Herbs and Trees.
15. Fructification in vegetable life.
16. Origin of low forms of animal life.
17. Insects and Reptiles appear.
18. Fishes, vertebrate life in the waters.
19. Birds, vertebrate life in the air.
20. Quadrupeds, vertebrate earth animals.

Third Order: Decad of Humanity.

21. Appearance of Man.
22. Material human body.
23. Human Soul conferred.
24. Mystery of Adam and Eve.
25. Complete Man as the Microcosm.
26. Gift of five human faces acting exteriorly.
27. Gift of five powers to the soul.
28. Adam Kadmon, the Heavenly Man.
29. Angelic beings.

30. Man in the image of God.

Fourth Order: World of Spheres.

31. The Moon.
32. Mercury.
33. Venus.
34. Sol.
35. Mars.
36. Jupiter.
37. Saturn.
38. The Firmament.
39. The Primum Mobile.
40. The Empyrean Heaven.

Fifth Order: The Angelic World.

41. Ishim--Sons of Fire.
42. Auphanim--Cherubim.
43. Aralim--Thrones.
44. Chashmalim--Dominions.
45. Seraphim--Virtues.
46. Malakim--Powers.
47. Elohim--Principalities.

ספר יצירה

48. Beni Elohim--Angels.

49. Cherubim--Arch-angels.

Sixth Order: The Archetype.

50. God. Ain Suph. He Whom no mortal eye bath seen, and Who has been known to Jesus the Messiah alone.

NOTE.--The Angels of the Fifth or Angelic World are arranged in very different order by various Kabalistic Rabbis.

Sepher Yetzirah   *Book of Creation*

THE THIRTY-TWO PATHS OF WISDOM

Translated from the Hebrew Text of Joannes Stephanus Rittangelius, 1642: which is also to be found in the "Oedipus Aegyptiacus" of Athanasius Kircher, 1653.

(These paragraphs are very obscure in meaning, and the Hebrew text is probably very corrupt.)

The First Path is called the Admirable or the Hidden Intelligence (the Highest Crown): for it is the Light giving the power of comprehension of that First Principle which has no beginning; and it is the Primal Glory, for no created being can attain to its essence.

The Second Path is that of the Illuminating Intelligence: it is the Crown of Creation, the Splendour of the Unity, equalling it, and it is exalted above every head, and named by the Kabalists the Second Glory.

The Third Path is the Sanctifying Intelligence, and is the foundation of Primordial wisdom, which is called the Creator of Faith, and its roots are AMN; and it is the parent of Faith, from which doth Faith emanate.

The Fourth Path is named the Cohesive or Receptacular Intelligence; and is so called because it contains all the holy powers, and from it emanate all the spiritual virtues with the most

ספר יצירה

exalted essences: they emanate one from the other by the power of the Primordial Emanation. The Highest Crown.) [1]

The Fifth Path is called the Radical Intelligence, because it resembles the Unity, uniting itself to the Binah, [2] or Intelligence which emanates from the Primordial depths of Wisdom or Chokmah. [3]

The Sixth Path is called the Mediating Intelligence, because in it are multiplied the influxes of the emanations, for it causes that influence to flow into all the reservoirs of the Blessings, with which these themselves are united.

The Seventh Path is the Occult Intelligence, because it is the Refulgent Splendour of all the Intellectual virtues which are perceived by the eyes of intellect, and by the contemplation of faith.

The Eighth Path is called the Absolute or Perfect Intelligence, because it is the means of the primordial, which has no root by which it can cleave, nor rest, except in the hidden places of *Gedulah*, [4] Magnificence, from which emanates its own proper essence.

The Ninth Path is the Pure Intelligence, so called because it purifies the Numerations, it proves and corrects the designing of their representation, and disposes their unity with which they are combined without diminution or division.

The Tenth Path is the Resplendent Intelligence, because it is exalted above every head, and sits on the throne of *Binah (the Intelligence spoken of in the Third Path)*. It illuminates the splendour of all the lights, and causes an influence to emanate from the Prince of countenances. [5]

The Eleventh Path is the Scintillating Intelligence, because it is the essence of that curtain which is placed close to the order of the disposition, and this is a special dignity given to it that it may be able to stand before the Face of the Cause of Causes.

The Twelfth Path is the Intelligence of Transparency, because it is that species of Magnificence called Chazchazit, [6] the place whence issues the vision of those seeing in apparitions. (That is the prophecies by seers in a vision.)

The Thirteenth Path is named the Uniting Intelligence, and is so called because it is itself the Essence of Glory. It is the Consummation of the Truth of individual spiritual things.

The Fourteenth Path is the Illuminating Intelligence and is so called because it is that *Chashmal* [7] which is the founder of the concealed and fundamental ideas of holiness and of their stages of preparation.

The Fifteenth Path is the Constituting Intelligence, so called because it constitutes the substance of creation in pure darkness, and men have spoken of these contemplations; it is that darkness

ספר יצירה

spoken of in Scripture, Job xxxviii. 9, "and thick darkness a swaddling band for it."

The Sixteenth Path is the Triumphal or Eternal Intelligence, so called because it is the pleasure of the Glory, beyond which is no other Glory like to it, and it is called also the Paradise prepared for the Righteous.

The Seventeenth Path is the Disposing Intelligence, which provides Faith to the Righteous, and they are clothed with the Holy Spirit by it, and it is called the Foundation of Excellence in the state of higher things.

The Eighteenth Path is called the Intelligence or House of Influence (by the greatness of whose abundance the influx of good things upon created beings is increased), and from its midst the arcana and hidden senses are drawn forth, which dwell in its shade and which cling to it, from the Cause of all causes.

The Nineteenth Path is the Intelligence of the Secret of all the activities of the spiritual beings, and is so called because of the influence diffused by it from the most high and exalted sublime glory.

The Twentieth Path is the Intelligence of Will, and is so called because it is the means of preparation of all and each created being, and by this intelligence the existence of the Primordial Wisdom becomes known.

Sepher Yetzirah   Book of Creation

The Twenty-first Path is the Intelligence of Conciliation and Reward, and is so called because it receives the divine influence which flows into it from its benediction upon all and each existence.

The Twenty-second Path is the Faithful Intelligence, and is so called because by it spiritual virtues are increased, and all dwellers on earth are nearly under its shadow.

The Twenty-third Path is the Stable Intelligence, and it is so called because it has the virtue of consistency among all numerations.

The Twenty-fourth Path is the Imaginative Intelligence, and it is so called because it gives a likeness to all the similitudes which are created in like manner similar to its harmonious elegancies.

The Twenty-fifth Path is the Intelligence of Probation, or Temptation, and is so called because it is the primary temptation, by which the Creator trieth all righteous persons.

The Twenty-sixth Path is called the Renewing Intelligence, because the Holy God renews by it all the changing things which are renewed by the creation of the world.

The Twenty-seventh Path is the Active or Exciting Intelligence, and it is so called because through it every existent being receives its spirit and motion.

ספר יצירה

The Twenty-eighth Path is called the Natural Intelligence; by it is completed and perfected the nature of all that exists beneath the Sun.

(This Path is omitted by Rittangelius: I presume by inadvertence.)

The Twenty-ninth Path is the Corporeal Intelligence, so called because it forms every body which is formed in all the worlds, and the reproduction of them.

The Thirtieth Path is the Collective Intelligence, and Astrologers deduce from it the judgment of the Stars and celestial signs, and perfect their science, according to the rules of the motions of the stars.

The Thirty-first Path is the Perpetual Intelligence; but why is it so called? Because it regulates the motions of the Sun and Moon in their proper order, each in an orbit convenient for it.

The Thirty-second Path is the Administrative Intelligence, and it is so called because it directs and associates the motions of the seven planets, directing all of them in their own proper courses.

Sepher Yetzirah   *Book of Creation*

Notes to THE SEPHER YETZIRAH

It is of considerable importance to a clear understanding of this Occult treatise that the whole work be read through before comment is made, so that the general idea of the several chapters may become in the mind one concrete whole. A separate consideration of the several parts should follow this general grasp of the subject, else much confusion may result.

This book may be considered to be an Allegorical Parallel between the Idealism of Numbers and Letters and the various parts of the Universe, and it sheds much light on many mystic forms and ceremonies yet extant, notably upon Freemasonry, the Tarot, and the later Kabalah, and is a great aid to the comprehension of the Astro-Theosophic schemes of the Rosicrucians. To obtain the full value of this Treatise, it should he studied hand in hand with Hermetic attributions, the "Isiac Tablet," and with a complete set of the designs, symbols and allocation of the Trump cards of the Tarot pack, for which see my translation of *The Sanctum Regnum of the Tarot*, by Eliphas Levi.

Note that the oldest MSS. copies of the "Sepher Yetzirah" have no vowel points: the latest editions have them. The system of points in writing Hebrew was not perfected until the seventh century, and even then was not in constant use. Ginsburg asserts that the system of vowel pointing was invented by a Rabbi Mocha in Palestine about A.D. 570, who designed it to assist his pupils. But Isaac Myer states that there are undoubted traces of pointing in Hebrew MSS.

ספר יצירה

of the second century. According to A. E. Waite there is no extant Hebrew MSS. with the vowel points older than the tenth century.

The words "Sepher Yetzirah" are written in Hebrew from right to left, SPR YTzYRH, Samech Peh Resh, Yod Tzaddi Yod Resh Heh; modes of transliteration vary with different authors. Yod is variously written in English letters as I, Y, or J, or sometimes Ie. Tzaddi is property Tz; but some write Z only, which is misleading because the Hebrew has also a true Z, Zain.

Sepher Yetzirah   *Book of Creation*

Notes to CHAPTER I

The twelve sections of this chapter introduce this philosophic disquisition upon the Formation and Development of the Universe. Having specified the subdivision of the letters into three classes, the Triad, the Heptad, and the Dodecad, these are put aside for the time; and the Decad mainly considered as specially associated with the idea of Number, and as obviously composed of the Tetrad and the Hexad.

1. *Thirty-two.* This is the number of the Paths or Ways of Wisdom, which are added as a supplement. 32 is written in Hebrew by LB, Lamed and Beth, and these are the last and first letters of the Pentateuch. The number 32 is obtained thus--2 x 2 x 2 x 2 x 2=32. Laib, LB as a Hebrew word, means the Heart of Man.

Paths. The word here is NTIBUT, netibuth; NTIB meant primarily a pathway, or foot-made track; but is here used symbolically in the same sense as the Christian uses the word, *way*--the way of life: other meanings are--stage, power, form, effect; and later, a doctrinal formula, in Kabalistic writings.

2. *Jah.* This divine name is found in Psalm lxviii. 4; it is translated into Greek as *kurios*, and into Latin as *dominus*, and commonly into the English word, *Lord*: it is really the first half of the word IHVH or Jehovah, or the Yahveh of modern scholars.

ספר יצירה

3. *Jehovah Tzabaoth*. This divine name is printed in English Bibles as Jehovah Sabaoth, or as "Lord of hosts" as in Psalm xxiv. 10. TzBA is an *army*.

4. *God of Israel*. Here the word God is ALHI, which in unpointed Hebrew might be God, or Gods, or My God.

5. *The Elohim of the Living*. The words are ALHIM ChIIM. Alhim, often written in English letters as Elohim, or by Godftey Higgins as Aleim, seems to be a masculine plural of the feminine form Eloah, ALH, of the divine masculine name EL, AL; this is commonly translated God, and means strong, mighty, supreme. Chiim is the plural of Chi--*living*, or *life*. ChIH is *a living animal*, and so is ChIVA. ChII is also *life*. Frey in his dictionary gives ChIIM as the plural word *lives*, or vitae. The true adjective for *living* is ChIA. Elohim Chiim, then, apart from Jewish or Christian preconception, is "the living Gods," or "the Gods of the lives, *i.e.,* living ones." Rittangelius gives Dii viventes, "The living Gods," both words in the plural. Pistorius omits both words. Postellus, the orthodox, gives Deus Vivus. The Elohim are the Seven Forces, proceeding from the One Divine, which control the "terra viventium," the manifested world of life.

6. *God*. In this case we have the simple form AL, EL.

7. *Sepharim*. SPRIM, the plural masculine of SPR, commonly translated *book* or *letter*: the meaning here is plainly "forms of expression."

8. *Numbers, Letters and Sounds.* The three Hebrew words here given are, in unpointed Hebrew, SPR, SPR and SIPUR. Some late editors, to cover the difficulty of this passage, have given SPR, SPUR, SIPR, pointing them to read Separ, Seepur, Saypar.

The sense of the whole volume appears to need their translation as Numbers, Letters and Sounds. Pistorius gave "Scriptis, numeratis, pronunciatis." Postellus gave "Numerans, numerus, numeratus," thus losing the contrasted meanings; and so did Rittangelius, who gave "Numero, numerante, numerato."

9. *The Ineffable Sephiroth.* The words are SPIRUT BLIMH, Sephiruth Belimah. The simplest translation is "the voices from nothing." The Ten Sephiruth of the Kabalah are the "Ten Primary Emanations from the Divine Source," which are the primal forces leading to all manifestation upon every plane in succession. Buxtorf gives for Sephiruth--predicationes logicae. The word seems to me clearly allied to the Latin spiritus--spirit, soul, wind; and is used by Quintilian as a sound, or noise. The meaning of *Belimah* is more doubtful. Rittangelius always gives "praeter illud ineffabile." Pistorius gives "praeter ineffabile." Postellus evades the difficulty and simply puts the word Belimah into his Latin translation. In Frey's Hebrew Dictionary BLIMH is translated as *nothing*, without any other suggestion; BLI is "not," MR is "anything." In Kabalistic writings the Sephiruth, the Divine Voices and Powers, are called "ineffbilis," not to be spoken of, from their sacred nature.

10. The classification of the Hebrew letters into a Triad, Heptad and Dodecad, runs through the whole philosophy of the Kabalah. Many

ספר יצירה

ancient authors added intentional blinds, suds as forming the Triad of A.M.T., Ameth, truth; and of AMN, Amen.

11. The Two Covenants, by the Word or Spirit, and by the Flesh, made by Jehovah with Abraham, Genesis xvii. The Covenant of Circumcision was to be an outward and visible sign of the Divine promise made to Ahraham and his offspring. The Hebrew word for circumcision is Mulah, MULH: note that MLH is also synonymous with DBR, dabar,--verbum or word.

12. Rittangelius gives "replace the formative power upon his throne." Postellus gives restore the device to its place."

13. *Abyss*; the word is OUMQ for OMQ, a depth, vastness, or valley.

14. My Hermetic rituals explained this Yetziratic attribution.

15. *The Lord the only God.* The words are ADUN IChID AL, or "Adonai (as commonly written) the only El."

16. *Seat.* The word is MOUN, dwelling, habitation, or throne.

17. *Lightning flash.* In the early edition the words "like scintillating flame" are used: the Hebrew word is BRQ. Many Kabalists have shown how the Ten Sephiroth are symbolised by the zig-zag lightning flash.

18. *God*; the Divine name here is Jehovah.

19. The text gives only RTzUAV ShUB--"currendo et redeundo," but the commentators have generally considered this to be a quotation from Ezekiel i. 14, referred to H ChIVT, the living creatures, kerubic forms.

20. The Spirit of the Gods of the Living. RUCh ALHIM ChIIIM; or as R. gives it, "spiritus Deorum Viventium." Orthodoxy would translate these words "The spirit of the living God."

21. AL ChI H OULMIM; "the Living God of Ages"; here the word God really is in the singular.

22. The Voice, Spirit and Word are QUL, RUCh, DBR. A very notable Hebrew expression of Divinatory intuition was BATh QUL, the Daughter of the Voice.

23. Formless and Void. THU and BHU; these two words occur in Genesis i. 2, and are translated "waste and void."

24. Note the order in which the primordial elements were produced. First, Spirit (query Akasa, Ether); then Air, Vayu; then Water, Apas, which condenses into solid elementary Earth, Prithivi; and lastly from the Water He formed Fire.

25. The first name is often written Ophanim, the letters are AUPNIM; in the Vision of Ezekiel i. 16, the word occurs and is translated "Wheels." ShRPIM are the mysterious beings of Isaiah vi. 2; the word otherwise is translated *Serpent*, and in Numbers xxi. 6, as "fiery serpents": also in verse 8 as "fiery serpent" when

ספר יצירה

Jehovah said "Make thee a fiery serpent and set it upon a pole." Kerubim. The Hebrew words arc ChIVTh H QDSh, holy animals: I have ventured to put Kerubim, as the title of the other Biblical form of Holy mysterious animal, as given in 1 Kings vi. 23 and Exodus xxv. 18, and indeed Genesis iii. 24. Bible dictionaries generally give the word as Cherubim, but in Hebrew the initial letter is always K and not Ch.

26. Three. In the first edition I overlooked this word *three*; and putting *and* for *as*, made four classes of serving beings.

27. This is verse 4 of Psalm civ.

28. Here follow the permutations of the name IHV, which is the Tetragrammaton--Jehovah, without the second or final Heh: IHV is a Tri-grammaton, and is more suitable to the third or Yetziratic plane. HVI is the imperative form of the verb *to be*, meaning *be thou*; HIV is the infinitive; and VIH is future. In IHV note that Yod corresponds to the Father; Heh to Binah, the Supernal Mother; and Vau to the Microprosopus--Son.

29. Note the subdivision of the Decad into the Tetrad--four elements; and the Hexad--six dimensions of space.

Sepher Yetzirah   *Book of Creation*

Notes to CHAPTER 2

This chapter consists of philosophic remarks on the twenty-two sounds and letters of the Hebrew alphabet, and hence connected with the air by speech, and it points out the uses of those letters to form words--the signs of ideas, and the symbols of material substances.

30. *Soul*; the word is NPSh, which is commonly translated *soul*, meaning the living personality of man, animal or existing thing: it corresponds almost to the Theosophic Prana *plus* the stimulus of Kama.

31. This is the modern classification of the letters into guttural, palatal, lingual, dental and labial sounds.

32. *The 231 Gates.* The number 242 is obtained by adding together all the numbers from 1 to 22. The Hebrew letters can he placed in pairs in 242 different positions: thus *ab, ag, ad*, up to *at*; then *ba, bb, bg, bd*, up to *bt*, and so on to *ts, tt*: this is in direct order only, without reversal. For the reason why eleven are deducted, and the number 231 specified, see the Table and Note 15 in the edition of Postellus.

33. *Non-existent*; the word is AIN, nothingness. Ain precedes Ain Suph, boundlessness; and Ain Suph Aur, Boundless Light.

34. *Body*; the word is GUP, usually applied to the animal material body, but here means "one whole."

ספר יצירה

Notes to CHAPTER III

This chapter is especially concerned with the essence of the Triad, as represented by the Three Mothers, Aleph, Mem, and Shin. Their development in three directions is pointed out, namely in the Macrocosm or Universe; in the Year or in Time; and in the Microcosm or Man.

35. The importance of equilibrium is constantly reiterated in the Kabalah. The "Siphra Dtzeniouta," or "Book of Mystery," opens with a reference to this Equilibrium as a fundamental necessity of stable existence.

36. *Heavens.* The Hebrew word Heshamaim HShMIM, has in it the element of Aesh, fire, and Mim, water; and also Shem, name; *The Name is IHVH*, attributed to the elements. ShMA is in Chaldee a name for the Trinity (Parkhurst). ShMSh is the Sun, and Light, and a type of Christ, the Sun of Righteousness. Malachi iv. 2.

37. *Were produced.* The Hebrew word BRA, is the root. Three Hebrew words are used in the Bible to represent the idea of making, producing or creating.

BRIAH, Briah, giving shape, Genesis i. 1.

OShIH, Ashiah, completing, Genesis i. 31.

ספר יצירה

ITzIRH, Yetzirah, forming, Genesis ii. 7.

To these the Kabalists add the word ATzLH, with the meaning of "producing something manifest from the unmanifested."

Emanation.	*Shin.*	*Aleph.*	*Mem.*
Macrocosm.	Primal Fire.	Spirit.	Primal Water.
Universe.	Heavens.	Atmosphere.	The Earth.
Elements.	Terrestrial Fire.	Air.	Water.
Man.	Head.	Chest.	Belly.
Year.	Heat.	Temperate.	Cold.

Sepher Yetzirah *Book of Creation*

Notes to CHAPTER IV

This is the special chapter of the Heptad, the powers and properties of the Seven. Here again we have the threefold attribution of the numbers and letters to the Universe, to the Year, and to Man. The supplemental paragraphs have been printed in modern form by Kalisch; they identify the several letters of the Heptad more definitely with the planets, days of the week, human attributes and organs of the senses.

39. These numbers have been a source of difference between the editors and copyists, hardly any two editors concurring. I have given the numbers arising from continual multiplication of the product by each succeeding unit from one to seven. 2x1=2, 2x3=6, 6x4=24, 24x5=120, 120x6=720, 720x7=5040.

40. In associating the particular letters to each planet the learned Jesuit Athanasius Kircher allots Beth to the Sun, Gimel to Venus, Daleth to Mercury, Kaph to Luna, Peh to Saturn, Resh to Jupiter, and Tau to Mars. Kalisch in the supplementary paragraphs gives a different attribution; both are wrong, according to clairvoyant investigation. Consult the Tarot symbolism given by Court de Gebelin, Eliphas Levi, and my notes to the *Isiaic Tablet of Bembo*. The true attribution is probably not anywhere printed. The planet names here given are Chaldee words.

ספר יצירה

41. The Seven Heavens and the Seven Earths are printed with errors, and I believe intentional mistakes, in many occult ancient books. Some Hermetic MSS. have the correct names and spelling.

42. On the further attribution of these Seven letters, note that Postellus gives: Vita--mors, Pax--afflictio, Sapientia--stultitia, Divitiae (Opus)--paupertas, Gratia--opprobrium, Proles--sterilitas, Imperium--servitus. Pistorius gives: Vita--mors, Pax--bellum, Scientia--ignorantia, Divitiae--paupertas, Gratia--abominatio, Semen (Proles)--sterilitas, Imperium (Dominatio)--servitus.

Sepher Yetzirah   *Book of Creation*

Notes to CHAPTER V

This chapter is specially concerned with the Dodecad; the number twelve is itself pointed out, and the characters of its component units, once more in the three zones of the universe, year and man; the last paragraph gives a recapitulation of the whole number of letters: the Supplement gives a form of allotment of the several letters.

43. It is necessary to avoid confusion between these letters; different authors translate them in different manners. Heh or Hé not be confused with Cheth, or Heth, Ch. Teth, Th also must be kept distinct from the final letter Tau, T, which is one of the double letters; the semi-English pronunciation of these two letters is much confused, each is at times both t and th; Yod is either I, Y, or J; Samech is simple S, and must not be confused with Shin, Sh, one of the mother letters; Oin is often written in English Hebrew grammars as Ayin, and Sometimes as Gnain; Tzaddi must not be confused with Zain, Z; and lastly Qoph, Q, is very often replaced by K, which is hardly defensible as there is a true K in addition.

44. Postellus gives *suspicion* and Pistorius, *mind*.

45. These letters are the initials of the 12 Zodiacal signs in Hebrew nomenclature. They are:

ספר יצירה

Teth	Telah	Aries	Mem	Maznim	Libra
Shin	Shor	Taurus	Oin	Oqereb	Scorpio
Tau	Thaumim	Gemini	Qoph	Qesheth	Sagittarius
Samech	Sartan	Cancer	Gimel	Gedi	Capricornus
Aleph	Aryeh	Leo	Daleth	Dali	Aquarius
Beth	Bethuleh	Virgo	Daleth	Dagim	Pisces

46. The month Nisan begins about March 29th. Yiar is also written Iyar, and Aiar: the Hebrew letters are AIIR.

47. The list of organs varies. All agree in two hands, two feet, two kidneys, liver, gall and spleen. Postellus then gives, intestina, vesica, arteriae," the intestines, bladder, and arteries; Rittangelius gives the same. Pistorius gives, "colon, coagulum (spleen) et ventriculus," colon--the large intestine, coagulum and stomach. The chief difficulty is with the Hebrew word MSS, which is allied to two different roots, one meaning *private, concealed, hidden*; and the other meaning *liquefied*.

48. The Elohim--Divine powers--not IHVH the Tetragrammaton.

Notes to CHAPTER VI

This chapter is a *resumé* of the preceding five; it calls the universe and mankind to witness to the truth of the scheme of distribution of the powers of the numbers among created forms, and concludes with the narration that this philosophy was revealed by the Divine to Abraham, who received and faithfully accepted it, as a form of Wisdom under a Covenant.

49. The Dragon, TLI, Theli. The Hebrew letters amount in numeration to 440, that is 400, 30 and 10. The best opinion is that Tali or Theli refers to the 12 Zodiacal constellations along the great circle of the Ecliptic; where it ends there it begins again, and so the ancient occultists drew the Dragon with its tail in its mouth. Some have thought that Tali referred to the constellation Draco, which meanders across the Northern polar sky; others have referred it to the Milky Way; others to an imaginary line joining Caput to Cauda Draconis, the upper and lower nodes of the Moon. Adolphe Franck says that Theli is an Arabic word.

50. *Happiness*, or a *good end*, or simply *good*, TUBH.

51. *Misery*, or an *evil end*, or simply *evil*, ROH.

52. This Hebrew version omits the allotment of the remaining six. Mayer gives the paragraph thus:--The triad of amity is the heart and the two ears; the triad of enmity is the liver, gall, and the tongue;

ספר יצירה

the three life-givers are the two nostrils and the spleen; the three death-dealing ones are the mouth and the two lower openings of the body.

53. *God.* In this case the name is AL, EL.

54. This last paragraph is generally considered to be less ancient than the remainder of the treatise, and by another author.

55. *The Lord most high.* OLIU ADUN. Adun or Adon, or Adonai, ADNI, are commonly translated *Lord*; Eliun, OLIUN, is the more usual form of "the most high one."

56. *Him.* Rittangelius gives "credidit in Tetragrammaton," but this word is not in the Hebrew.

57. *Tongue.* The verbal covenant.

58. *Speech.* The Hebrew has "upon his tongue."

59. The Hebrew version of Rabbi Judah Ha Levi concludes with the phrase, "and said of him, Before I formed thee in the belly, I knew thee." Rabbi Luria gives the Hebrew version which I have translated. Postellus gives: "He drew him into the water, He rose up in spirit, He inflamed him in seven suitable forms with twelve signs." Mayer gives: "Er zog sie mit Wasser, zundet sie an mit Feuer; erregte sie mit Geist; verbannte sie mit sieben, goss sie aus mit den zwolf Gestirnen." "He drew them with water, He kindled them with fire, He moved them with spirit, distributed them with seven, and sent them forth with twelve."

Sepher Yetzirah   *Book of Creation*

Notes to the Thirty-Two Paths of Wisdom

1. The Highest Crown is Kether, the First Sephira, the first emanation from the Ain Suph Aur, the Limit-less Light.

2. Binah, or Understanding, is the Third Sephira.

3. Chokmah, Wisdom, is the Second Sephira.

4. Gedulah is a synonym of Chesed, Mercy, the Fourth Sephira.

5. Metatron, the Intelligence of the First Sephira, and the reputed guide of Moses.

6. This word is from ChZCh, a seer, seership. Chazuth is a vision.

7. This word means "scintillating flame."

The "Thirty-two Paths of Wisdom" refer to the Ten Sephiroth and the Twenty-two letters, each supplying a type of divine power and attributes. In my *Introduction to the Kabalah* will be found a diagram showing how the Paths from Eleven to Thirty-two connect the several Sephiroth, and are deemed to transmit the divine influence. Some teachers of Occult Science also allot the Twenty-two Trumps of the Tarot Cards to the twenty-two Paths.

ספר יצירה

ספר יצירה

Sepher Yetzirah   *Book of Creation*

TGS Publishers

22241 Pinedale Lane
Frankston, Texas 75763

HiddenMysteries.com
903-876-3256